Go Fishing

with Jack Charlton

Additional material by
Chris Dawn
Features Editor *Angling Times*
and
Fred J. Taylor

COLLINS
in association with
Channel Four Television

First published in 1983 by
William Collins Sons & Co Ltd
London · Glasgow · Sydney · Auckland
Johannesburg · Toronto

9 8 7 6 5 4 3 2 1

© THORN EMI Video Programmes Ltd 1983

Based on the THORN EMI Video Programmes series
Go Fishing with Jack Charlton, broadcast on Channel Four
Television and released on video cassette, devised and
produced for TEVP by John Drewry/Filmscreen

This book was art directed and edited for Collins by
John Drewry Associates, London

Editorial and Series Consultant Chris Dawn
Editorial Consultants Len Cacutt, Fred J. Taylor

Illustrations by Johnathan Wolstenholme
Fish species illustrated by Dr Dietrich Burkel

ISBN 0 00 411778 6
Typesetting by Videoset Ltd
Colour origination by York House Graphics
Printed in Italy by Imago Publishing Ltd

Welcome to Go Fishing! Whether you're a raw beginner, or an experienced angler, I'm sure you'll find something to interest you in this book. It's the story of a series of angling programmes we made for television; and although the schedules were pretty hectic, I haven't enjoyed myself so much since being a member of the England World Cup winning team, way back in 1966.

I believe angling to be one of our great sports, standing alongside soccer; and it's about time that the stars of the sport were afforded the credit they deserve. That's what these programmes are all about. I'm no expert, but quickly learn when given the chance. So I snapped up the opportunity to go fishing with some of the great names in the sport. The great float angler Ken Giles took me barbel fishing on the Severn: they didn't prove easy to catch that day – but I learnt a lot. Denis White and Dick Clegg showed me how to catch bream and roach on a reservoir – a water which, incidentally, stands just a few minutes from my home. Then there was that magic trip off the Devon coast with skipper Lloyd Saunders. I'll never forget that one, especially as I caught my first conger eel!

Perhaps my first love is trout fishing, so I couldn't wait for a day on Rutland Water, with Bob Church. He makes it look so easy, but once Bob had revealed his tricks of the trade I was knocking fish out just as fast. Thanks, Bob, for a great day's fishing, and we've been the best of friends ever since. Sea trout are one of our most fascinating fish, and very exciting to fish for – let alone catch. I felt privileged to fish with river keeper Ray King on Devon's river Taw, especially when he caught a fine sea trout, right on dusk. We fished on through the night, when I caught one as well.

However, there's no doubt in my mind that the finest trip of all was to Scotland, on the river Tay. Everything seemed against us. The river was in nearly full flood, but thanks to Jess Miller, of Dunkeld House Hotel, we pulled off the impossible and caught a fresh-run 18 lb salmon. What a fight! And what an experience, which you can read all about in this book. But I didn't get much of it to eat myself by the time the others had wolfed it up!

All through this book we've tried to show you exactly what the anglers are doing, and then explain why; and I believe we've got it right!

World-class matchman, Ken Giles, has figured time and again in the richest prizes in angling. He is a member of the Shakespeare Super Team, Birmingham AA, and has been selected to fish for England on many occasions.

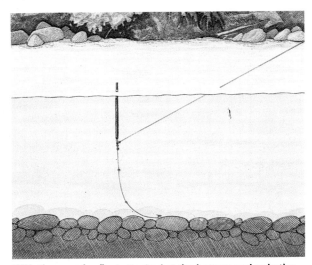

With the waggler float attached at the bottom end only the line can be made to sink, avoiding surface and wind drift. The bait can be set to drag bottom behind the float's path. Used for longer range fishing. The shot needs to be concentrated around the base of the float to provide casting weight. The rest of the shot are equally spaced down the line.

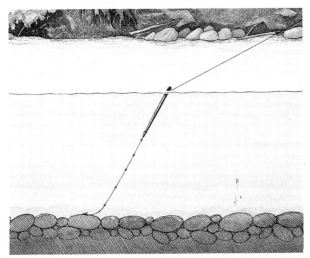

Attached top and bottom, the stick float may be held back to allow the bait to precede the float. Shots are more evenly spaced for better control of the tackle and better bait presentation. Used for short and medium range in rivers and also chosen according to the strength of current and wind.

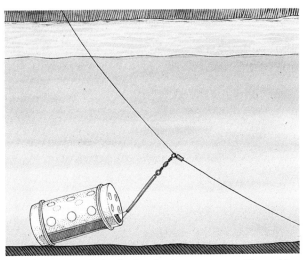

The block-end swimfeeder is a feed presenter, and is used for accurate baiting of the swim near the hook in running water. The holes allow bait to escape around the hook bait area. Also acts as a casting and leger weight. The running swivel enables a bite to be detected, without obstruction.

River Coarse Fishing

There's a fascination about moving water that I've never been able to shake off. I can remember as a lad leaning over a bridge on the Northumberland moors, and spending hours watching the small trout playing in the current. It wasn't until later that I was able to afford a rod and start fishing for them, but those early experiences made me an angler.

In this country we're lucky to have so many fine waters to choose from. Whether you're a river fisherman, or prefer still-water, there's a fishery for you. The river Severn is among the best in the land. It holds just about every species in its 220 miles (350 km), from the source in the Welsh mountains down to the tidal estuary below Tewkesbury. The best coarse fishing of all is from Bridgnorth, in Shropshire, downstream to Stourport. This is barbel country, but there's also a good head of chub, dace, roach and even salmon. Bream don't come into the reckoning until we reach Worcester, where the river starts to widen and deepen.

The original stock of barbel were introduced into the river by the *Angling Times,* in conjunction with the Severn River Board, way back in 1956. I'm told that a total of 509 fish from the river Kennet went in the fast middle reaches. Well, they obviously found the Severn to their liking because in many areas they are now the dominant species.

I'm afraid that not everyone has welcomed the barbel. Because these fish have driven out many of the river's native species, match anglers have had to rely more and more on the barbel to win; and that means using an item of tackle called the swimfeeder, which you'll learn more about later. The barbel have become used to the splash of the swimfeeder, associating it with food, so the float anglers haven't had a look in, which is a shame because you need much more skill to control a float in a fast river like the Severn than you do to cast out a heavy swimfeeder.

One of the most skilful float fishermen around is Ken Giles. Ken has been fishing and winning matches on the Severn for years now; and perhaps understands the river and its moods better than anyone. Ken agreed to take us to one

The most widely used reel is the open-faced fixed spool, which takes a lot of headaches out of casting. The principle is that the line comes off the spool at right angles, making over-runs impossible. A slipping-clutch mechanism prevents fine line breakage.

Soft pouch catapult for shooting groundbait and loose feed to the hookbait area.

of his favourite stretches of the river between Bewdley and Stourport. It's a beautiful length where the trees on the wooded banks overhang the water. Mind you, the banks are steep, so I only hope that everyone can get down without falling in the water.

We found Ken with some difficulty, standing at his peg. It always seems to me that only the lazy anglers sit on their baskets. The more serious fishermen stand up to make sure they don't miss a single bite. Already Ken had his net in the water, and by the way it pulsed in the current it must have contained a number of fish.

'Morning, Jack! How are you?' Ken greeted me as though we'd been buddies all our lives. That's the sort of friendly guy he is. He's well known on the match-fishing scene for being a real gentleman.

Ken was floatfishing the waggler across the far side of the river, on a fast shallow. The sun shining on the water through the trees gave him perfect visibility. I watched for a few seconds as he skilfully controlled the float down the swim. Then the float dived away and he was playing a fair chub. He didn't waste much time either, bringing the fish to his hand and lifting it out of the water. It was around a pound, which is the average size for this part of the river.

Ken explained the three basic methods for fishing the Severn. 'First, there's the stick float method where the float is attached top and bottom. Then, there is the waggler, where the float is attached by the bottom end only. Finally, there's the swimfeeder, which is really a form of legering. The stick float is used for fishing the nearside of the river. If it were cast too far, the angler could never control it properly. For fishing the far side of the river, you'll need the waggler.'

Ken showed me his float, a nicely-finished length of peacock quill, known in the trade as a straight waggler. Some of the ones for slower water have a small insert of cane or quill in the tip for extra sensitivity. For casting across a wide river, like the Severn, the shot need to be concentrated around the base of the float to provide the casting weight. The rest of the shot are spaced equally down the line to give the bait a delicate, natural presentation.

Well, Ken made it all look so easy. When you watch him closely you realise that everything he does is to a pattern. First, he casts out with an overhead cast, swinging the float behind and then punching the rod forwards, stopping it at the one o'clock position. When the float reaches the swim he's fishing, he feathers the line to let it gently hit the water, with the minimum of disturbance. Next, he closes the bale arm with a quick turn of the reel handle, and puts the rod down on the well-positioned rod rests. He picks up his bait catapult and fires out a pouch of loose casters taken from the pocket of his bait apron. It's all done so quickly and smoothly that the float has hardly travelled any distance down the swim before Ken is holding the rod again. Now, both hook-bait and loose feed are travelling down the swim together, attracting the chub into the swim.

It's pretty obvious that the angler's catapult is a pretty essential item in this style of fishing. Without it, Ken would never be able to feed the far side of the river. Ken showed me his, and explained how the pouch has air holes to offer less air resistance when fired. He's also plugged the end, so that it floats if he accidentally drops it in the river. All clever stuff!

There seems to be a purpose behind everything that Ken does. His rod rests are high up, so that when the rod is placed on them the line is not drooping in the river. This means that when he picks up the rod to strike, there's the minimum of line on the water.

One thing mystified me, so I asked Ken why he had so much float showing above the water, when I have been taught to shot it right down. Ken explained, 'The boils on the water surface tend to suck the float under, giving you false bites, so you'd be continually striking at nothing. This way, with plenty of float showing, you strike only when you've got a bite. Like that . . . '

Another chub was played across the river.

The hook came out so easily that I wondered if the chub had been properly hooked. Ken just laughed, 'I'm using barbless hooks. They are kinder to the fish, and much more pleasant to use. For a start, if you hook yourself in the finger, it doesn't mean a trip to the casualty department – they drop straight out: but if you keep the pressure on when playing the fish, they rarely come loose. The only fish you occasionally lose is a dace, when they spiral in the current.'

Line spin can be quite a problem in fast water, especially when the angler uses two maggots, or casters, on the hook. Ken gets round that one by threading one caster up the shank of the hook, blunt-end first; and then hooking the second one on, through the narrow end. That gives a perfect presentation, yet prevents the two baits spinning like a propeller on the retrieve and kinking the line.

Ken Giles is a perfectionist in everything he does. His floats, which he makes himself, are some of the finest around. I asked to see them, and Ken produced a box big enough to sit on. We opened the top to see rows and rows of stick floats, made from balsa and cane. Some are all

Two casters on a No. 16 barbless hook. Barbless hooks make it easier to bait with fragile casters.

A selection of waggler floats for different water conditions. Fine-tip inserts are likely to be used more in slow or still waters for sensitive bite detection. Bodied wagglers are used for long range or when the wind is a problem

black, for fishing when there's a sheen on the water. Others have a fluorescent orange top, for fishing on a dull day, or when the swim is surrounded by trees – like the swim Ken was fishing.

The next section of the box holds Ken's wagglers – so-called because they tend to *waggle* through the swim when fished on a loose line. These are always attached to the line with a rubber float adaptor, which allows Ken to quickly change floats if wind or light conditions demand, without interfering with the shotting. The heavier antenna-floats in the final section of the box have balsa bodies, loaded with brass inserts. Ken explained that these are for distance fishing on still or slow-moving waters, such as you find in Eastern England.

Well, we still hadn't caught a barbel. Ken tried both caster and bronze maggots on the hook, feeding regularly every cast (very important that) without success. So I went to look further upriver, where some anglers were fishing with swimfeeders; and it was here that I saw my first barbel – a beautiful bronze fish, packed with muscle and power. Barbel don't keep too well in keepnets, so I watched while the captor gently returned it to the river.

At the next peg to Ken, Clive Smith was reluctantly trying the swimfeeder. Clive is another household name in match-fishing circles, and has a very big reputation. He was selected to fish for England in 1981 on the Warwickshire Avon. Unfortunately, the river came up in spate and the French beat us into second place.

Like Ken, Clive is a float fisherman first and foremost, but he knows that as a match angler

A selection of swimfeeders including block-ends, open-ends and feeder-links. Hole sizes vary and choice of size depends upon the nature of the swim and the speed of the current.

Barbel
Lean, powerful-bodied fish built to hug the bed of a fast-flowing river. Has four barbules, used to seek out food. Snout has drooping shape, ideal for rooting around among weeds and stones on river bed, hunting for diet of aquatic animals, weed and worms. Prefers clean gravel runs, between banks of streamer weed or weir pools. Introduced to number of English rivers; found mainly in Thames valley, southern chalkstreams, Yorkshire Ouse system, River Severn, Hampshire Avon and Dorset Stour.
Tackle: Needs to be strong. Swimfeeder or leger with line 4-7 lb (2-3 kg).
Bait: Maggots, sweetcorn, hempseed, cheese or luncheon meat.

Chub
Chunky fish with greedy appetite: grows to 9-10 lb (4-4.5 kg), but typically good specimen is 3 lb (1.5 kg). Thrives best in fast-flowing water where there is bankside cover. Smaller chub live in shoals. Larger chub become solitary. Widely distributed in England. Absent from Ireland, and scarce in most of Scotland, west Wales and south-west Cornwall. At its fighting best late in season.
Tackle: Snaggy water needs heavy tackle. Waggler float works best where bottom is clean.
Bait: Casters, cheese, lobworms, tares, luncheon meat.

Dace
Delicate fish, average weight 4-8 oz (110-225 gm) from swiftly-flowing rivers such as Hampshire Avon or Wye. Fond of fast water and aerated shallows, but can be found in all rivers in shoals. Feeds off the bottom. Often mistaken for immature chub: distinguished by spreading dorsal and anal fins. Dace has concave fins, whereas chub has rounded, convex fins.
Tackle: Light float tackle trotted down the current.
Bait: Maggots, casters, bread. Or smaller grub baits. Can be fished for with either wet or dry flies in smaller sizes.

Gudgeon

Small bottom species. Similar body shape to barbel, but just two barbules, one at each top corner of mouth. Body is almost straight from mouth to anal fin. Prefers running water, over gravel or sandy bottom; but can be caught in shallow lakes. Feeds on minute organisms, and withstands high degree of pollution. Shoals in vast numbers.
Tackle: Very light float tackle laid on to the bottom.
Bait: Maggots, small worms.

Roach

Found in lakes, rivers and ponds throughout British Isles. A shoal fish in both still and running waters. Feeds on minute water creatures, worms and some plants. Small waters tend to produce stunted fish, while fish over 1 lb (0.5 kg) come from large gravel pits, reservoirs or fast-flowing rivers. Tell from rudd by dorsal fin positioned directly above pelvics, and both jaws of equal length.
Tackle: Light float tackle carefully controlled.
Bait: Maggots, casters, bread punch, hempseed, tares, wheat.

Rudd

Deeper body than roach, and tends to golden scale colouring. Fins are much brighter red, and eye is brilliant red (rudd is often called 'Red Eye'). Found in England, Wales and Ireland: Rudd prefers still waters and slow-running rivers, especially quiet slacks and backwaters. Surface feeder; rises freely to floating baits on a still evening. Feeds best in summer.
Tackle: Self-cocking float with slow-sinking bait.
Bait: Bread flake, maggots, and all baits suitable for roach. Rise freely to dry fly on summer evenings.

he's got to go prepared for every eventuality; and that means carrying swimfeeder gear in his basket. One of his main objections is the way lost swimfeeders have littered many swims with heavy line. This has spoilt the swims for the float fisherman. It also makes the job of feeding the swim extremely simple, removing a lot of the skill from fishing.

Clive was using a green Drennan feeder, which merges nicely with the river bottom. He showed me how the bait trickles out of the holes in the feeder, to entice the fish towards the angler's hook. One of the feedermen's tricks is to enlarge the holes in the feeder to allow more bait to escape. On the Severn, the best feed is a mixture of hemp and caster which, unlike maggots, would not escape from the feeder without a great deal of assistance from the current. So, it's particularly important to open up the holes.

Clive told me to first bait the hook with a single caster, and then fill the feeder. Do it the other way round and by the time you're ready to cast out the feeder might be empty. This is especially important with maggots.

Most feeder fishermen aim to get as much bait in the swim as possible at the start of their session. They do this by using an extra-large swimfeeder, packed with bait. This is then repeatedly cast out into the river, until the angler is satisfied that he has laid a carpet of several pints of bait on the river bed. It's generally considered bad luck to catch a barbel too quickly. If the fish are already in the swim, they could become scared. Better for the fish to move into the swim after an hour or so, and settle on the feed.

Hempseed, fed in conjunction with casters, attracts and holds fish in the swim, particularly bigger species such as chub and barbel. On fast flowing rivers, the angler may need several pints of both baits.

Tony Davies, a member of the Shakespeare Super Team, discusses a specimen roach. The tackle included a closed face reel. In these reels, the line spool is enclosed and the pick-up mechanism is not exposed. These reels are ideal for fine line techniques used by match anglers. There is little danger of line peeling off in strong wind and becoming tangled.

You'll need heavy tackle for swimfeeder fishing, to take the strain of casting something that could weigh as much as 3 oz (0.1 kg) when packed with bait. Line should be around 6 lb (2.7 kg), as compared with around 2 lb (0.9 kg) for float fishing, and the rod a heavy-legering job rather than the 12 and 13 ft (3.6 and 3.9 m) carbon rods now favoured by float fishermen. Some of the most successful feeder anglers favour the use of a soft-actioned rod, which actually allows the barbel to hook itself. On no account should the angler touch the rod until the barbel is banging away on the end. If you strike too soon and retrieve your tackle, you'll just pull the empty feeder into the barbel and scare them off.

The feeder rod needs to be positioned upright, in the air, almost like a beach rod. This keeps the line off the water, and makes bite indication very easy. With a soft-topped rod there's no need for a quivertip. You can't miss the pull of a hungry barbel; and with the heavy weight of the swimfeeder anchoring the bait to the bottom, the barbel will usually hook itself. You can always make your swimfeeder heavier by adding ski-leads, which can now be bought from any tackle shop.

There was just one more method that we hadn't seen in use, and that was the stick float. Tony Davies was using one in a steadier swim, up river from Clive. It's not a method to catch barbel, or even chub, particularly in summer. But for the smaller species like roach and dace, it's unbeatable.

Tony was fishing the stick float in conjunction with a closed-face reel – in contrast to the more conventional open-faced fixed spool favoured by Ken and Clive for their styles of fishing. He prefers it for close-in work because it's tangle free. He showed me how he releases the bail arm by just pressing the centre button. The line is then free to leave the spool. It's great for casting, too. All you do is depress the button and cast out the stick float with an underarm swing, replacing the finger to brake the float when it hits the water. Then you let the float work down the swim, controlling the line with the index finger. When you want to reel in, you simply wind the reel handle, and a small pin in the reel picks up the line for the retrieve.

It all seemed so simple as I watched Tony run his float delicately down the current. He was fishing only just beyond his rod top, so he had perfect control at all times. Sometimes he held the float back for a second and at other times, he let it run through at the speed of the current. He explained that you had to find out how the fish wanted the bait.

The stick float was originally devised by Lancashire match angler Benny Ashurst, for catching roach as the bait fell through the water. With a balsa top and heavier cane base, the original stick float pivots in the water to allow a perfect presentation. Since then, other anglers have come up with their own ideas, including the now popular wire-stemmed stick float which rides rougher water far better, such as on the Severn.

With the stick float, the angler can hold the float hard back so that the bait is travelling in front of the float. This method is particularly useful in cold weather when the fish are lethargic, and not inclined to chase a bait. In contrast, the waggler float, fished bottom end only, is always travelling in front of the bait, so the float disappears when the fish grabs hold.

Tony showed me his shotting pattern – a series of No 4 and No 6 shot neatly spaced out down the line in the traditional 'shirt button' style. This allows for perfect bait presentation, and while we were talking the float stabbed under with a lovely bite.

It proved to be a roach, a perfect specimen with silver scales tinged with blue and fins of deep red. We returned it to the river and both watched it glide away across the shallows to the deeper water.

A selection of stick floats. The lower inserts are made of a heavier density wood that the buoyant upper half. Greenheart is probably the most popular hard wood used for inserts. These floats are invariably attached to the reel line by float caps top and bottom or double-rubber as it is often described.

Still Water Coarse Fishing

Although I manage Sheffield Wednesday football team I live in Worsborough, very close to the Yorkshire mining town of Barnsley. Coarse fishing is a strong tradition in my part of the world. It's a great escape for anglers, who perhaps spend most of their working lives in industrial surroundings. At the weekend, there's nothing better to get rid of the coal dust or the factory grime than an outing to the Lincolnshire Fens, or the river Trent.

One lake we're particularly proud of is Worsborough reservoir. It may not look as pretty as some stately home waters, but I bet it holds as many fish. I happen to live within casting distance of the water and my favourite evening stroll takes me right along the banks. Mind you, there's also a nice pub at the end!

When these fishing programmes were first suggested, I knew that Worsborough reservoir had to be a priority. For a start, it would prove to all those Southerners that Yorkshire isn't just slag heaps and cloth caps!

In Barnsley, we have one of the finest match-fishing teams in the country – if not the finest. Every one of the team's members is a star in his own right, yet when it comes to the team they all pull together. We're like that in Yorkshire. The two most well-known members of the squad are Dick Clegg, who runs a tackle shop in the town, and Denis White, a big blond-haired boy who injured his back in a mining accident and now works above ground when he's not match-fishing.

Dick and Denis, plus Tom Pickering and Keith Hobson, are the stalwarts of the Barnsley Blacks – the name they call themselves. Some people say that the name arose because of the coal-mining connection. Others, because it referred to taunts from rival Lancashire anglers that their casters were from the black shiner fly, which produces a worthless bait – so they stuck to maggot. But whatever the origin, it's a black day for the other anglers in a match when the Barnsley lads are on form.

Dick Clegg *(left)*: Captain of the invincible Daiwa Barnsley Blacks. Dick led his team to win the Embassy Championship in 1982, for the second time.

Denis White *(right):* A member of the famous Barnsley Blacks, shows us a specimen perch that he'd just caught while swingtip fishing. Denis has been picked to fish for England on many occasions.

They've won the Angling Times Winter League twice, Division One National, Captain Morgan Cup, Benson and Hedges and Embassy Challenge to name just a few.

The team's local river is the Trent, where they've scored some impressive victories. But that still means a 50-mile (80 km) drive down the motorway, so they do all their practising for the big events on Worsborough reservoir, where they really are unbeatable. Any teams drawn against them in the Captain Morgan Cup on this water are on a hiding to nothing.

The match record holder for the water is Denis White, so I wasn't surprised to see Denis hauling-in a fair bream when I arrived at the water.

The popular match man's swing tip. This hangs from the rod tip and indicates bites by rising to the pull of a taking fish. A fish coming towards the rod will be indicated by a dropping of the swing tip. The effects of wind may be reduced by setting the extreme end of the tip on to the surface. Always sit in a position so that you can see the tip, with the rod positioned 45 degrees to the wind.

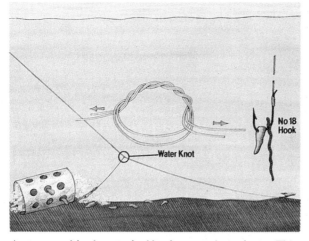

No 18 Hook

Water Knot

An open-end feeder attached by the water knot shown. This does not run freely on the line as does the swivel attachment.

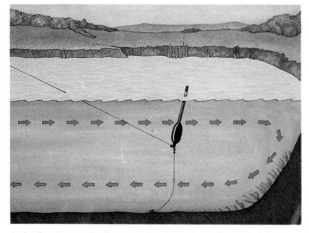

In high winds a float may be pulled out by the surface flow while the bait tends to be caught in the undertow and strives to move in the opposite direction. There are times when casting into the teeth of the wind has the effect of pulling the bait outwards when the undertow takes charge.

Denis was swingtipping with a standard two-piece, 10 ft (3 m) rod and long fibre-glass swingtip that hung just above the water. That morning, bites were shy and Denis had to watch like a hawk for the slightest movement. I was interested in his end tackle, which included an open-ended swimfeeder. This took the place of a leger weight, but placed a small carpet of feed right next to the hook bait. The hook was a size 18, baited with a redworm and a maggot, tied to a 4 ft (1.2 m) long leader.

The whole set-up looked complicated to a non-expert like me, but Denis assured me that it was one of the easiest methods for a beginner to use and catch big fish, 'This is a fairly cheap outfit for someone just starting to fish', explained Denis, 'and they can fish very efficiently with it. Floatfishing a lake like this would be far more difficult with a float. With a good ripple on the water, you tend to get a considerable movement. The surface water often moves in a different direction to the water on the bottom, so that a beginner trying to floatfish would find that his float was being dragged one way, with the wind, while his bait was being pulled another way underwater. This is known as undertow, and is quite common on big waters; but legering with a swimfeeder, as I'm doing, eliminates the problem.'

The swimfeeder is a simple item of tackle, yet perhaps one of the most effective devised. You fill it with maggots, casters, or whatever you are using on the hook, then hold them in place with cereal groundbait. Denis was at pains to point out to anglers not to pack the bait in too tightly. If you do, there is always the chance that the feeder will not empty properly in the swim, and any bait left in the feeder might come out on the retrieve, spreading it over a much larger area, which is precisely the opposite of what you are trying to achieve.

Of course, not every angler can ever hope to be as skilful as Denis, but watching anglers of his class can improve your fishing ability. I was impressed how Denis cast his feeder to the same spot every time, by lining up a marker on the opposite bank. He let the swimfeeder sink with the reel bale arm open, so that it ended up on the same spot of lake bed.

To supplement the feed – as bream are hungry fish – Denis fired a ball of bait from his catapult. The left arm was locked straight, with the catapult held at right angles. A clean fire, and the ball sped through the air to hit the water some 30 yards (27 m) from the bank.

Bream fishing demands accurate groundbaiting, and for that the consistency of the groundbait must be just right. For a start, never mix up too much groundbait at one go, as it will usually dry out by the time you come to use it. Always add water to your groundbait, never the other way around. That way you can control the mixture and, if you are using maggots as feed, two tiny squatts are the best, as they hold the shoal longer.

Never tip too many maggots into your groundbait bowl at once. They will either cling to the outside of the ball, so attracting small fish into the swim, or they will break up the ball in midflight.

Top match anglers like Denis normally use the brown or golden crumb cereal feed to take the maggots to the fish. If they want the ball to break up more slowly, or fire further, they add some white crumb which clogs the bread – but then only as much as is needed.

Originally built as a compensation reservoir to top up the local canal, Worsborough has never fished better thanks to an explosion in the numbers of skimmer bream. Match weights of 25 lb (11.2 kg) plus are regularly taken, while pleasure catches can top 50 lb (22.4 kg). Some of the best swims are off the dam wall, where the angler is about 8 ft (2.5 m) above the water. It doesn't make for easy swingtipping, but Denis was proving the method works. The bream had now gone quiet, their place being taken by a shoal of hungry perch, and they were good-sized fish as well, with several up to the pound mark.

It was during lunch that the bream moved back into Denis's outside swim. He switched to gozzer on the hook – an ultra-soft maggot that has to be bred in the dark – and was soon into fish that scaled up to 3½ lb (1.6 kg).

To demonstrate the variety of methods that work on a typical still-water, such as Worsborough, tackle dealer Dick Clegg was using a carbon pole, worth over £500. The pole performed well on the inside swim, which Dick had baited with golf-ball sized offerings of squatts and crumb.

Dick's choice of the roach pole was just another way of beating surface drift, where the wind-driven surface water moves the float against the subsurface current. This undertow is actually caused by the waves beating on the shore, the water being pushed down underneath and back out into the lake. By using the roach pole he could hold the bait in position, untroubled by surface currents.

The perch seemed as interested in taking Dick's bait as they had been earlier in Denis's offering of worm and maggot. Many waters have suffered from perch disease, but so far Worsborough does not seem to have been affected.

Groundbait made up into tight balls and mixed with inferior hookbait samples can be thrown accurately to the hookbait area to break up and form a feed carpet. The consistency of the mix can be adjusted to allow the break-up to occur on impact or to disintegrate more slowly on the bottom. Here, a typical shelf or drop-off is baited. Heavy, tightly squeezed balls of bait may be thrown a long way by hand but many anglers today use catapults for both distance and accuracy.

The versatile hard-pouch catapult which may be used for maggots, casters, all kinds of seed bait, and groundbait pastes.

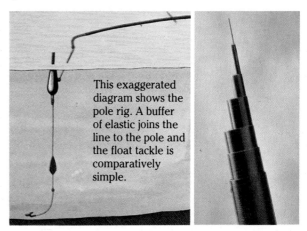

This exaggerated diagram shows the pole rig. A buffer of elastic joins the line to the pole and the float tackle is comparatively simple.

The carbon fibre pole. The ultimate tool in still-water or very slow-moving water for fixed line, close range fishing. Some of these poles are as long as 30 ft (9m). No reel is used. The line is attached to the pole tip and the pole may be dismantled section by section when fish are being landed.

Hookbait selections. It has been said that anything you can eat yourself will make a hook bait for a fish at some time or other! Here are shown several kinds of maggots (bronze, pinkies, reds, squatts), and casters in various shades of their development, and seed baits (far right) comprising hemp, tares and sweet corn. All these are referred to as particle baits because they are made up of large numbers of identical particles. There are many others including beans, peas, sultanas, elderberries and stewed wheat. Their effectiveness lies in an ability to stimulate fish into feeding by weaning them on to the large numbers introduced as free offerings. This is usually referred to as loose feeding. Such simple baits as bread, crust, paste, lobworms, brandlings, boiled potatoes and cheese should not be overlooked. They remain both popular and effective for what is usually referred to as pleasure fishing.

Other specialist baits include crayfish, mussels, slugs, waspgrubs, sausage and luncheon meat. All succeed at different times and on different waters. The last-mentioned are, perhaps, more popular with the big fish specialists or specimen hunters.

Dick demonstrated how he held the pole comfortably for many hours at a time, 'The ideal position is to hold the pole across your leg, and balance it with the right hand', he explained. 'When you get a bite you just lift the pole with both hands.'

He then struck into a fair fish which stretched the end elastic as it ploughed about the swim. This elastic actually plays the fish, and finally tires it ready for the net. To net the bream, Dick had to ship the pole down to its final joints as I sat on the wall and watched.

Like all top match anglers, Dick takes an amazing quantity of bait with him when he goes fishing. To tempt the roach that Worsborough holds, Dick had fed another swim, closer in, with casters. At this point, it's worth pointing out that all top match anglers always feed two or more swims – one close in and the other further out. The far – invariably bream – swim, is fed with balls of groundbait. The near – roach – swim, is fed with loose feed such as sinking casters, the chrysalid stage of the bluebottle.

Though casters have presently lost their popularity to bronze maggots, they are still a very effective bait on a water where they have not been over-used. One theory behind the decline of the caster is that anglers insisted on throwing away their unused ones, which were often stale, into the water. So the fish became wary of them.

If you buy casters from the shop, never keep them more than a week, and then only in the 'fridge. If you prepare your own, you'll have to pick them off quickly while they are still light coloured. In warm weather they quickly darken as the fly inside starts to form, becoming useless as bait when they no longer sink, because they float away from the swim and may take the fish with them.

Maggots still catch as many fish as ever, but there are always current vogues about colour. At present, red maggots are the 'in' thing, often appearing to the fish as a tiny worm, or perhaps even a bloodworm. Bronze maggots have been popular for years, but now there's some talk about the danger to health, due to the chrysodine dye used to stain them.

For small fish, the pinkie is unbeatable. This little maggot, with a pinkish sheen, is actually the larva of that unpleasant fly, the greenbottle. But they keep very well in the 'fridge for weeks, provided you keep them dry. Damp pinkies can crawl up the side of a house, and you don't want the health inspector round! These, too, can be dyed bronze to be fished in conjunction with bronze hook maggots. On some waters, the fish prefer them dyed a deep shade of bronze; on other waters a lighter shade is more effective. Ask your bait dealer to dye them for you. Home dying is a messy, and perhaps hazardous business.

Squatts, the smallest of the maggots, are the larvae of the house fly, and extremely effective for bream fishing. Unlike other maggots, they don't attempt to crawl away into the bottom mud, and stay where you've thrown them for the bream to find; and a shoal of bream can stay in the swim for a long time while clearing up a few pints of squatts.

Whatever bait you use, always ensure that it's clean. Riddle out any old dead maggots, rubbish, or sawdust, replacing them in clean bran or maize meal: ask your tackle dealer for some.

Our discussion was broken by another bite on Dick's delicate pole float. The bristle disappeared and this time it was a fine roach that was hooked. I could hardly see the hook in the lips of the roach, it was so fine. Dick showed it to me—a size 22 barbless tied to just a 1 lb (0.5 kg) line bottom. Was there any need to use such a tiny hook, I asked? Dick assured me that there was, especially on a well-fished water where the fish have become shy of larger hooks.

How did he tie such a small spade-end hook to his line? Again Dick laughed and proceeded to show me how to tie the spade-end whipping knot with his deft fingers. I think I'll stick to buying my own already tied!

Then, as if to demonstrate still further that you don't need a big hook to land a good fish, Dick hooked into a tench . . . an unusual fish for Worsborough reservoir. Dick admitted that it was one of the few he'd ever caught from the water. The tiny hook had been swallowed, so Dick carefully held the tench while he gently used the disgorger. The plastic disgorger slid down the line and on to the hook shank, making unhooking an easy process. The little hook easily came away, but the shock of being caught made the tench lose some spawn. Even in late July, this tench had not yet spawned, which makes a bit of a mockery of our close season. Tench, along with carp, generally fare better in more southern waters where water temperatures are higher, so perhaps there's a case for different close seasons for different areas.

The spade-end hook remains the most popular with match anglers, as it can be neatly tied on to any breaking strain of line. Eyed hooks are normally reserved for specimen hunters, where a bulky knot will not interfere with delicate bait presentation. If you're after bream, or other largish fish, always choose a forged hook for its extra strength. For smaller fish, such as roach and dace, a fine-wire hook allows better

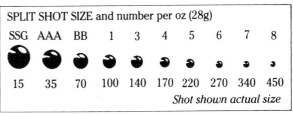

The simplest and speediest method of tying a spade end hook. Many anglers use this knot to tie up hook links in advance. Some prefer to tie the hook directly to the reel line and avoid intermediate knots.

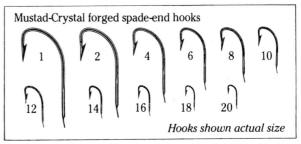

Mustad-Crystal forged spade-end hooks

| 1 | 2 | 4 | 6 | 8 | 10 |
| 12 | 14 | 16 | 18 | 20 | |

Hooks shown actual size

Size chart for Crystal, forged, spade-end hooks. From No. 1, hooks get smaller down to size 20.

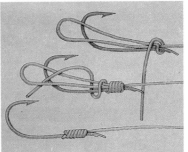

SPLIT SHOT SIZE and number per oz (28g)

SSG	AAA	BB	1	3	4	5	6	7	8
15	35	70	100	140	170	220	270	340	450

Shot shown actual size

A disgorger is used to remove hooks from fish that have taken the bait too deep. The disgorger homes in on the hook by following the line and a gentle push-and-pull draws the hook out leaving the fish unharmed.

penetration and less damage to the bait. Most match anglers now seem to prefer the barbless hook, as it makes unhooking so much easier. If you accidentally snag one in your keepnet or sleeve, then it just falls out, unlike the barbed variety. Various patterns of hooks become popular. Ask your tackle dealer which are the best, and then buy a box or packet. You can never go fishing with too many hooks but, if they become damp, you'll have to throw them away, as the slightest touch of rust on the point will blunt them. Therefore, always keep hooks in watertight packets, or little boxes smeared with grease.

The light south-westerly wind that had been blowing into the dam, creating perfect bream conditions, had dropped away, so Denis White was now trying a float for the first time in the day. Like all top match fishermen, Denis loves using a float when conditions are right. He'd chosen a waggler, where the line is attached by the bottom end only. It is either passed through the eye, or through an interchangeable float adaptor. The bulk of the shot was pinched round the base of the float to provide casting weight, with just a couple of smaller shot pinched on the line below halfway, between float and hook. On the hook length were two tiny dust shot − No. 8's − as 'tell-tales'. Denis explained that if a fish were to pick up his bait from the bottom, and so take up the weight of the shot, the float would rise in the water by the amount that would normally be cocked by the shot. These are called lift bites, and are made easier to spot by having a thin piece of cane inserted into the tip of the float, painted in various black and white bands. Cane is a more dense material than quill, requiring less shot to take it under, so it rises all the more easily when a fish takes up the weight of the shot. If you see the white band below the coloured tip appear out of the water, then you strike.

The same approach can be used for 'on the drop' fishing. Here, the fish takes the bait before it ever reaches the bottom. By using a sensitive float with a painted tip, it's again possible to see a lift bite as the float fails to settle when the fish intercepts the bait.

For distance fishing, Denis uses much larger floats made from peacock quill, with balsa bodies. The extra body allows the float to carry more shot around its base, and so be cast much further. Another alternative is to use a float with the extra weight already built into the base of the float. These are known as zoomers, for their casting ability, and require very little shot down below. A similar effect can be achieved by winding lead wire round the base of the float.

Waggler floats are often attached to the line at a set depth by what is known as trap-shotting. In other words a shot pinched on the line above and below it secures it without a float cap. The float rides freely on the line and a little space must be left between the shots to allow the float to fold on the strike. Quick changes are made easy by the separate rubber adapter attachment shown. Floats may be replaced without having to remove shots and dismantle tackle.

Most top match anglers always shot their floats from the hook upwards. In other words, they decide how the fish want the bait by the shotting pattern they choose. Then they select the float to match the water and wind conditions at the time. This is easy to achieve if you use a float adaptor which allows you to change floats quickly and easily.

After casting out a waggler float on still-water, it's important to sink the line as quickly as possible, to prevent the tackle being blown out of position by the wind. You can do this by plunging the rod top below the water surface, and winding a few turns of the reel handle. Some brands of line sink better than others and, again, your tackle dealer will advise. Alternatively, if you know that you'll be waggler fishing, you can soak your line in washing-up liquid the night before to remove all traces of grease so that the line will sink.

Denis explained that it was no good floatfishing blind. You had to know the depth of water you were fishing, and for that you needed a plummet, which was basically a lead weight with an eye for the line at one end, and a piece of cork to take the hook on the other. 'Start by setting the float to the depth you think might be correct,' said Denis, 'then thread the hook line through the plummet, nicking the hook into the bottom cork. Gently swing the lead out to where

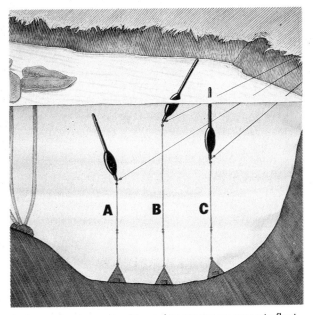

A plummet or heavy lead is used to ensure an accurate float setting. If the float is not set deep enough, it will sink (A). If it is too deep, the float will lie flat on the surface or not cock properly (B). You have judged the depth correctly when the float just shows (C). Remember the depth can vary in any given area.

disappearing in one particular area, then it's a good bet that there's a hole on the bottom − another place worth fishing.

By its very nature bream fishing is a waiting game. We'd seen Denis start in fantastic style, catching bream and perch on the swingtip. Now he was sticking to the float and catching quality roach. In complete contrast crafty Dick had started on his inside swim, taking a variety of smaller fish, but all the time he had been feeding his other swim further out. Now, he was legering with a quivertip right on his earlier feed, and the bream were there in force.

He was offering the fish a choice of two baits, by fishing the double-hook method popular in the North. We watched as the finely-tapered tip curved round with a bite. He had hooked a big hybrid that had the line singing in the rod rings, but this fish just didn't want to throw in the

you want to fish. If the float sinks, then you're fishing too shallow, so move the float up the line until it is visible. Then you know your hook bait is going to be on the bottom. You can usually feel the plummet land on the bottom as the rod tip straightens.'

'Today I'm fishing my float about 12 in (0.3 m) overdepth, which is helping to steady the bait. If the float starts to move with the surface drift, then it may pay to add another small shot near the hook.' he explained.

Sometimes, it proves difficult to cast a heavy plummet very far out into the lake that you're fishing, so another way of finding the depth is by simply pinching a swanshot just above the hook. It's still not easy to cast, but can be useful to find the shelf in a lake which is where most fish, such as bream, feed. If the float disappears, then you know that you've cast into too deep water. Keep reeling back, and slackening the line until the float reappears. When it finally lays flat on the surface, you know that you are in too shallow water, so somewhere between the two positions is the shelf. When the float first starts to cock perfectly, you've hit the shelf; and that's where to bait.

Another use of the plummet is to find a deep hole in a lake or river bed, where fish will often lie at the bottom. Again set the plummet to the depth of the water, and cast it out. If it keeps

Denis White shows all the concentration of the top-flight matchman as he adjusts the line after casting. Note how the trays of maggots are placed at hand.

Tench

Hard-fighting species caught mainly at the start of the season. After July they become more difficult to catch. Found among weed beds or lily pads, in shallow lakes. Respond well to pre-baiting, or swim clearing.
Tackle: Needs to be strong. Float or swimfeeder with 3-6 lb (1.5-3 kg) line.
Bait: Sweetcorn,   worms, bread, maggots.

Bronze bream

Mainly found in still or slow-moving water, in East Anglia, the Midlands and Southern England. Prefer a muddy bottom where the shoal can root around. Clues to feeding bream are colour in the water and tiny needle bubbles bursting on the surface.
Tackle: Legering with a swing, or quivertip.
Bait: Bread, redworm, maggots, tares. Plenty of groundbait required.

Common carp

Largest fish found in still waters. Best fished for at night in summer. Can be caught either on the bottom, or from the surface. Carp are shy fish and have a reputation of being hard to catch. Tough fighters when hooked.
Tackle: Needs to be strong with line 7-12 lb (3-5.5 kg). Free line or leger.
Bait: Bread, worms, sweetcorn, luncheon meat, high protein specials.

towel. The rod straightened as the fish made good its escape. In between bream bites, I asked Dick to explain the virtues of the quivertip. His was made from an 18 in (0.45 m) length of solid glass, sanded down to a very fine tip, and whipped in to the end of the leger rod. Some anglers prefer to buy separate quivertips that can be screwed into the end ring like a swingtip. This way, the strength and length can be varied to suit conditions.

The quivertip is much easier to set up than a swingtip, and less prone to be blown about by the wind. It does offer more resistance to a biting fish, but bites can be picked up just as easily if you watch it closely. Like the swingtip, which shoots straight out with a bite, don't wind too much tension into the tip. You want just sufficient tension to pick up a drop-back bite, should a taking fish move the lead as well.

Dick's end tackle for bream fishing was the same simple paternoster used earlier by Denis. The hook tail is tied to the main line by a five-turn water knot, and the bomb attached to the end of the reel line. A ½ oz (14 gm) bomb is normally sufficient for most legering, but in really windy conditions you may need to go up to 1 oz (28 gm).

By five o'clock the light had deteriorated, even though the fishing was as good as ever. The warm breeze ruffling the water surface had stirred the bream into feeding, but all good things have to come to an end.

We lifted both nets from the water. There was very little to choose between the two catches, but overall Denis had caught bigger fish, with bream and roach-bream hybrids to 3½ lb (1.6 kg). Dick joked that this was because he had been pole fishing for most of the day!

Denis also included some fabulous roach and perch in his near 30 lb (13.5 kg) net, but Dick could claim the most unusual fish of the day, with his tench. All the fish were safely returned, perhaps to swim away and be caught another day.

Perch

Predatory fish, fond of weir pools in rivers, but grow to heaviest size in deep still-waters. Ponds may contain stunted perch. Found all over the British Isles.

Tackle: Leger or livebait rig.
Bait: Live minnows, lobworms, maggots.

A selection of leger and spinning leads including coffins, spirals, barleycorns, bombs and bullets. These come in many different sizes to cope with current speed, searching out swims, holding the bottom, rolling in the current, and adding weight for casting distance and range.

23

Sea Wreck Fishing

You can't beat the sea. As soon as I breathe that salt tang through my nostrils, boyhood memories come flooding back. I started fishing as a lad, from the rocks at Newbiggin on the north-east coast. It was great, but I really struggled for decent tackle. I can remember making my own Scarborough reel from an old tea chest, and my rod must have seemed like a broomstick compared to today's shiny examples. But I caught fish, and that's what it's all about. Not giants, but tasty cod and haddock which all the family appreciated!

Recently I went sea-fishing with a few others, aiming to catch some really big stuff . . . conger, ling, pollack, cod, turbot and even shark.

To catch these sort of fish we had to go well offshore where the water drops away to 30 fathoms (55 m) or more. Taking us out to the fishing grounds was charter-boat skipper Lloyd Saunders from Dartmouth, Devon. Lloyd makes his living from taking anglers to some of the best sea-fishing gounds in the West Country, on his well-equipped boat Saltwind II.

For the best sport, we wanted to fish over one of the many war-time wrecks that litter this part of the English Channel. The trawler fleets of the world have cleaned out much of our inshore waters, leaving them barren and fishless. But many fish have been driven into the wrecks where they can live and feed in relative safety from the trawlers' nets.

We set out on a fantastic morning — the sea so calm it looked like a blue carpet stretching away to the horizon. We started away early from the quayside before the holidaymakers were up and about; only those noisy herring gulls were there to see us off.

Mackerel feathers come in many different forms. They are used in a team of six and often lowered on a hand line that is taken down by a heavy pear lead. Very often all six feathers will be taken by the aggressive mackerel in dense shoals and sufficient for a whole day's fishing may be taken in a few short minutes.

A very sharp knife is essential for filleting mackerel. Make the first cut through to the backbone just behind the pectoral fin. Cut towards the tail. Hook mackerel fillet through the tail end, pulling the hook eye through at the same time.

The other half of mackerel can be used for conger or ling, by feeding the hook through the mouth, and out through the hard part of the head. Fresh blood released into the sea will attract predators.

Squid can be used whole for big fish such as conger or cod. Alternatively, having opened out and scraped off the outer skin, the firm flesh can be cut into thin white strips, and when hooked onto feathers, offer a tempting bait for sea bream.

Even skipper Lloyd was amazed by the forecast. It was just force one north-west, which means really no wind at all. Only the previous week, Lloyd was battling his boat against severe gales. Lloyd pointed out a small basking shark finning on the top. These are the fish that often come right into holiday beaches, scaring the bathers out of the water; yet they are perfectly harmless.

To a working skipper like Lloyd, days like this are virtually a miracle. Lloyd will tell you that in one month he lost two-thirds of his bookings through windy weather, yet the day we went out there was none at all. It was just as well, as I hadn't brought my anti-seasickness tablets.

To supplement their incomes from boat hire, many of the more successful charter-boat skippers sell their catches on the market. The anglers are allowed to take away just two fish – but remember they could weigh around 20 lb (9 kg) apiece. So when the weather is set fair, the boat skipper must quickly cash-in with the fish.

The day before our trip, Lloyd had gone out to deep waters to hit a new wreck for 2,200 lb (990 kg) of ling, but with every other boat finding fish too, market prices had slumped to 25 pence per stone. That meant a bonus of just £39 in his pocket, after a long and expensive trip.

We were not so ambitious, and headed for an inshore wreck that had been well cleared of ling and pollack by commercial fishermen and anglers alike; but it still provided the occasional big conger eel. The initial flush of enthusiasm for long-distance wreck fishing has died away and, besides the boredom of a five-hour boat journey out to the wreck, catching one 25 lb (11.3 kg) ling is very much the same as catching one inshore.

The inshore wreck we were going to fish – off Start Point – provided the opportunity to try for several different species. The conger we wanted are always present, ready to feed at the right state of the tide.

Lloyd Saunders is one of the top wreck skippers in the south-west, quietly taking advantage of the fishing opportunities around him. He splits his time between hunting for bass with live sand-eel close to the rocks, drifting the Skerries Bank for plaice and turbot, or fishing the many wrecks. Lloyd still believes there are at least another 50 wrecks waiting to be discovered between the Eddystone Light and Berry Head.

Lloyd is the current holder of the coalfish record, with a 33-pounder (14.9 kg) – his second over 30 lb (13.5 kg). His best pollack is a creditable 22 lb 13 oz (10.3 kg) and he's had many more big ones on light tackle, which is one of his specialities.

Before Lloyd or any of us aboard could even think of catching such fish, we stopped to try to catch some bait, and there's no finer bait for deep-sea angling than fresh mackerel: in summer, mackerel is the fish which the predators – such as ling and conger – will be hunting anyway. We were just making it easy for them.

All you need for catching mackerel is a string of bright feathers tied to your reel line. It must be the simplest fishing there is. Even I could catch mackerel this way. Clip just sufficient lead to the end of your line with a swivel. If you can reach the bottom easily, then it's the right amount. Then quickly raise your rod and drop it, to work the feathers in the tide. The mackerel can be deep, and other times they show high in the water. You've just got to find them by experimenting. When mackerel are shoaling really thick, they'll stop your lead dead. Then it's a case of reeling in a full string of six, with a fish on each hook!

We fished over the famed Skerries Bank; mackerel were chasing sand-eels over the shallow sand banks there, and we managed to foul-hook a few of the eels. We also caught a few whiting on white feathers; like all sea fish, whiting are predatory.

When the bait box was full, we moved on to find the wreck, laying in some 40 fathoms (75 m) off Start Point. There was quite a fair bit of tide running.

To find the exact position of the wreck, Lloyd uses a Decca Navigator and his echo sounder. And like all professional skippers, he keeps a little book with the exact Decca numbers of the wrecks. When his receiver tells him he's in the area, Lloyd switches on the echo sounder and sweeps the sea-bed. This is always an exciting time, and everyone wants to be in the wheelhouse to watch. A really sensitive sounder like Lloyd's will also tell him what fish, if any, are present.

Lloyd had been to this particular wreck so many times that the boat seemed to know its own way. As we crossed the various Decca radio 'lanes' we knew we were right on course. As the final numbers clicked up in the wheelhouse, Lloyd flicked on the sounder, and there was the wreck.

To us, above the water, the wreck appeared as just a black smudge on a piece of paper. But the experienced boat skipper can tell which way the boat is laying to the tide, and where the fish are to be found. With the tide still running hard, we couldn't anchor up until slackwater, so we started by fishing for pollack.

Pollack is the main predator on the wreck. Small pollack live inshore by harbour walls, or

Even on fine days oilskins are to be recommended. Rain or saltwater spray can be unpleasantly cold at sea and it is better to be safe than sorry.

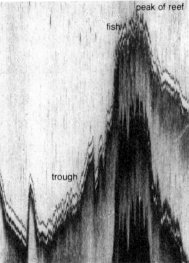

peak of reef

fish

trough

The echo-sounder chart can show the position of a wreck in deep water. The really sensitive sounder can show what fish, if any, are present.

A selection of swivels – essential items of equipment for sea fishing. Swivels prevent line twist, and can be used for quick tackle changes. There are some available that contain five or more ball bearings in their housings.

A typical heavy duty wire trace with intermediate swivels, effective for conger. The wire resists the sawing of predator's teeth.

Conger
The most ferocious and powerful predator on the wreck; difficult to bring to the boat. Conger grow to well over 100 lb, and call for the heaviest of tackle.
Bait: Fresh mackerel or pouting.

Ling
Bottom feeder found in great numbers on West Country wrecks. Huge catches can be made on a virgin wreck. Blows its swim bladder in deep water, spoiling the fight.
Bait: Mackerel strip or baited pirk.

Cod
Big cod frequent wrecks all year round, feeding on the shoals of sprat and pilchard. North Sea wrecks tend to be dominated by cod, whilst West Country wrecks often have the biggest specimens.
Bait: Artificial eels, pirks, white feathers.

Red bream
Grows larger than the black bream, and has the black thumb-print behind the gill case. Found only in western waters off Devon and Cornwall.
Bait: Baited feathers, strips of squid.

John Dory
A solitary species found no further north than the English Channel. Caught mainly by accident. It has huge jaws that are telescopic. Great to eat.
Bait: Mackerel or pirks.

Black bream
A Mediterranean species that moves into English Channel waters in summer. Good to eat and sporting to catch, the black bream spawns over wreck or reef. Best caught on light tackle.
Bait: Strips of squid.

Pouting
Pouting grow to a medium size over a wreck, feeding on the rich food available. Not a sporting species, they still grab a fish bait meant for bream or pollack.
Bait: Mackerel strip, squid.

Turbot
The prime fish of the wrecks caught often by accident when an angler's bait lands in the sand gulley that builds up around an underwater obstruction. Wreck turbot are some of the biggest caught.
Bait: Fresh mackerel fillet or sand-eel.

Blue shark
Shark tend to hang around wrecks, attracted by the shoals of food fish available. The blue shark is our most common predator in summer, often snatching pollack from an angler's line.
Bait: Fresh mackerel.

along rocky cliffs, until they have to move further out to sea to find more food. Wreck pollack usually start around 8 lb (3.6 kg), and go up to 20 lb (9.0 kg). Double-figure weights are the norm rather than the exception.

One feature of Lloyd's boat is a bait well, for live fish such as sand-eel. Pollack prefer nothing better! The sand-eel must be fished on a long trace tied to a wire boom, then it can be worked in the tide. Next to me, Tony was using a trace of 18 feet (5.4 m), with a 6/0 hook on the end. The hook is threaded through the lip and then just nicked in the belly, to ensure that the eel stays good and lively.

However, it wasn't a pollack that took Tony's bait, but a greedy pouting. I was amazed that such a small fish could swallow such a large bait.

Also on the trip was Chris Dawn – features editor of the Angling Times. Chris has been on deep-sea trips many times before, and I was hoping that he'd show me the ropes. But early on I became caught in the wreck. That's one of the ever-present hazards of wreck fishing – once you allow your hook or lead to swing amongst the mass of rusted metal on the bottom, you can usually kiss it goodbye.

Chris caught a fair pollack of 9-10 lb (4.0 to 4.5 kg) on an artificial sand-eel known as the Red Gill. These rubber eels were invented by a chap called Alex Ingram, down in Mevagissey, and they have revolutionised sea fishing. They can be bought in different sizes and colours. Some days a small black eel will work, while on other days you'll need one of bright orange. Chris was using a luminous green one, and the pollack seemed to like it.

The appeal of the artificial sand-eel lies in the action of its tail, which vibrates in the water in a very natural manner. When the tide is running hard, the eel works best on a long trace of 12 ft (3.6 m) or more, but on neap tides the length of the trace should be reduced, otherwise you'll suffer from tangle.

Lloyd was content to let the boat drift with the tide across the wreck. We were trying for pollack – winding up our sand-eels slowly through the water. For this style of fishing, it's much easier if everyone fishes from the same side of the boat, so they can pay their sand-eels out in the tide. Chris showed me how to hold the tail of the eel tight, with the lead in the water, until the skipper gives the word to start fishing. Once you've released the lead, you should let the eel follow. Do this the other way round, and the long trace will simply tangle round the main line. As in all boat fishing, you'll be using a multiplier reel coupled with a rod of 20 lb (9 kg), 30 lb

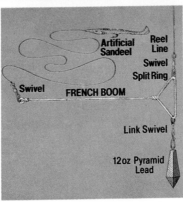

Artificial sand-eels come in many sizes and colours and today's modern plastic and rubber versions have built-in wriggles.

Typical pollack or cod rig, fished with an artificial eel. The french boom prevents tangling the main reel line with the trace.

Pollack
The most sporting fish found on the wreck. Pollack move off the reefs to the deeper-water wreck marks when they reach a good size. Responsible for more broken lines than any other fish.
Bait: Artificial eel, mackerel fillet.

A regular two piece boat rod for use with lines around 30 lb (13.5 kg) breaking strain. Screw winch fittings hold the reel secure. Note the special runners replacing traditional rod rings.

The reel used for most boat fishing at sea is the simple multiplier. This holds a great deal of heavy line and has harness attachments for fighting big fish.

Playing a big fish at sea calls for a special technique usually referred to as pumping. The harness holds the reel upright; the rod butt is placed into a butt pad. To regain line the angler waits for an opportunity to lower the rod point and wind in the slack. He then lifts the rod and pumps the fish towards him, being prepared at all times to release pressure if the fish makes a sudden dash. Having pumped the fish towards him, he lowers the rod again and takes in more slack before repeating the process once more, making sure his thumb feeds the line evenly across the spool, to avoid line build up and tangle. This procedure is continued until the fish is ready to be boated, gaffed, or drawn into the landing net.

Strong tides may require lead weights of 2 lb (0.9 kg) or more. Two shapes are popular, the conical and the hydrodynamically shaped sea anchor. Smooth-shaped leads are less likely to foul wrecks.

(13.5 kg) or perhaps 50 lb (22.5 kg) line class. Once you've released the reel spool by putting it out of gear, control the eel's descent through the water by thumbing the spool. When it hits bottom the lead will stop, then start to wind it slowly back. If you let the lead hit bottom without thumbing the spool, expect a big 'bird's nest' of line which will jam the reel.

I watched Chris bring his eel up through the water by steadily turning the reel handle. It's really a form of spinning: when the eel reaches the level where the pollack are feeding, you can expect your first bite. This was really exciting stuff. Chris told me what to expect: 'The rod tip bends over, and the reel becomes more difficult to turn. But, whatever you do, don't strike or stop reeling-up. The pollack, which has swum up behind the bait, will simply spit it out. Keep reeling and the fish will be yours, provided you've remembered to adjust the star drag on the side of the reel. All pollack dive straight back to the wreck and you must let them go, to a certain extent, otherwise they will smash your line. So, don't have that drag screwed up too tightly. After that first powerful run, you should have your pollack beaten'.

Well, it was about time I caught a fish. The skipper was taking the boat back over the wreck to anchor uptide, so our lines could fish into the base of the wreck. It looked a complicated business, because if he anchored too close, our lines would be streaming over the top of the wreck and we'd be fishing on the wrong side.

One of the best positions to bottom fish is from the stern of the boat. This way you can fish with just the right amount of lead, and not catch anyone else's tackle. Tangles are a fact of life in deep-sea fishing, especially when one angler doesn't bother to put on a heavy enough lead.

All the fresh air had made me hungry, so while I shared some sandwiches with the crew, my mackerel-baited rod was left to fish for itself. Of course, that's the best way to get a bite.

Suddenly a cry went up: 'Watch your rod, Jack', and there was definitely a fish banging away at the end. I thought it might be my first conger eel. Chris Dawn insisted on giving me instructions as I played the fish to the top: 'Pump the rod, adjust the clutch, keep reeling'. This sea-fishing lark is all pressure; just let me get Chris onto a football field!

Well, it wasn't a conger, but a fine ling — my first ever. I suppose it's the big brother of those tiny rockling I used to catch from the pier when I was a kid. The swim bladder had blown from its mouth — that's what happens when you catch fish from great depths.

With the tide still running hard, we needed

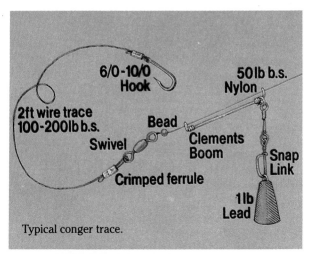

6/0-10/0
Hook

50lb b.s.
Nylon

2ft wire trace
100-200lb b.s.

Bead

Swivel

Clements
Boom

Snap
Link

Crimped ferrule

1lb
Lead

Typical conger trace.

Lloyd Saunders, the skipper, shows a beautiful red bream, caught on a simple Paternoster rig with baited feathers.

Courtesy of Angling Times

2 lb (0.9 kg) of lead to reach the bottom. But when it slackened off, we needed only half a pound. To fish for conger and ling, you need a wire trace attached to a 30 lb (13.5 kg) or 50 lb (22.5 kg) line. The hook can be anything from a 4/0 to a 10/0, with the main line running through a Clements boom to take the weight. To take the continual strain of winding up what feels to me like a sack of potatoes – from 200 ft (60 m) of water – you should use a butt pad. This goes round your waist, with a rubber cup to take the end of the rod, and eliminates a lot of the strain, and even potential injury, from deep-sea fishing.

The next fish I hooked really did call for that butt pad. It was a conger, and fought all the way to the boat. The record stands at an incredible 109 lb (49 kg), taken off Plymouth in 1976, but Lloyd told me that eels of more than 160 lb (72 kg) have been taken on long lines by commercial fishermen. A 200 lb (90 kg) eel has been netted by a trawler. I just hope that I never hook one that big.

While I was congratulating myself on my conger, Lloyd's dad, Bill, started to huff and puff over what appeared to be a very big fish. Lloyd picked up his biggest gaff, and ordered everyone out of the way. Down in the translucent depths, the grey shape of a conger spiralled upwards.

'Conger, and a fair one. Clear the decks!' rapped Lloyd in a serious voice. One mighty swipe with the gaff, and 40 lb (18 kg) of writhing, chomping eel soared skywards bound for the fishbox. You don't mess around with eels of that size, which are quite capable of removing a hand or a foot.

Some smaller 'strap' conger came aboard before the tide stopped completely. Lloyd speedily rigged up some baited feathers, Paternoster style, to catch some hard-fighting red bream, to 3 lb (1.4 kg) or so. Then the tide started to run the other way, and all too soon it was time to up-anchor. Still, it was only a 90 minute trip back to harbour – preferable to the much longer journeys back from the offshore wrecks. Many West Country boats now fish round the Channel Isles.

On the ride home we all mucked in, gutting the catch and swabbing down the boat. Skippers appreciate this sort of help, especially when they've worked hard to put you onto fish. Back on the harbour front, other boats had landed blonde ray, plaice and flatfish – in complete contrast to our conger, ling and pollack. There can be few grounds in the south-west that offer such a wide variety of fishing – and also such an able skipper as Lloyd.

And at the end of a fabulous day's fishing, there wasn't a green face to be seen.

Ray King, fly fishing on the river Taw. He is searching out the quieter waters above a run.

River Trout Fishing

When we talk of river trout, of course, we are onto a wide subject, and there are many differences in approach and technique between the trout of – say – a peaty northern river, and the chalk streams of the south of England. There are differences, generally speaking, in the size and quality of the fish, and in many cases their beginnings are unrelated. Some southern chalk stream trout begin their lives in hatcheries, whilst most northern stream trout are wild fish, spawned and reared naturally in the river. We may all look forward to catching big brown trout at times, and there are many big still-waters in the British Isles where both wild and stocked brown trout grow to a great size, but always there is the urge to come to terms with the wild, native brown trout of our rivers and streams. The fish seldom grow to any great size but they are beautiful to see, exciting and difficult to catch, and delicious to eat.

I was lucky indeed to find myself on Devon's river Taw in search of wild brownies, and I believe that all who love to fish would find pleasure in those lovely surroundings.

The rivers Taw and Torridge are very popular with tourists, but it's still possible to get away from the hustle and bustle of it all by asking discreet questions and doing some advance reconnaissance; and there is more to it than that. The wild life of the area is an attraction in itself, and there are times when the sight of a heron or kingfisher may serve to distract an angler, but perhaps that's how it should be!

These two small rivers are natural trout streams, and both of them have a run of sea trout in summer. A few salmon head upstream from time to time, too, and I think it's fair to say that few small rivers can boast of salmon, sea trout *and* quality brown trout. In keeping with most good river traditions the sea trout are not usually fished for until night time, and the pools where they congregate should really be left alone during daylight. Fortunately, browns and sea trout tend to have different lies and it is possible to fish for both species at their appropriate times, without problems.

Ray King, the river keeper, took me in hand and pointed out many spots in the stream where browns might lie. I recognised the little pools below the stony shallows as being choice feeding spots, and I could see areas of overhanging foliage where trout might seek shelter and shade. Trout are cautious creatures, and for much of their time they simply lie in wait for food to come to them, in the current. They may tuck themselves away close to the bank in inaccessible spots, or rest up below a rippling shallow, leisurely sucking in insects when the mood takes them. Occasionally they may go on a wild feeding spree, when food is abundant, but for much of the time they are easily scared by rod flashes and shadows. They bolt in terror at a plop on the surface, and a clumsy cast with a fly rod will put them down at once. The dry or floating fly has to be presented so that it lands gently on the surface of the water. Then it has to

Brown trout
Britain's native species. Common in rivers and lakes in West and Northern Britain, but also now being artificially introduced into many still-water reservoirs. Feed on insects, worms and small fish.

Sea trout
The sea trout is basically the brown trout which has evolved a migratory way of life. The colour is invariably silvery with dark brown spots.

Typical fish-holding spots in a game fish river include deep pools below fast shallows, shady overhangs, boulder and rock sanctuaries, streamy runs and lively eddies. During the summer trout tend to lie quietly in the deepest water, moving into more oxygenated shallows and faster runs to feed in the early morning and late evening.

Although fly casting is different from all other kinds of casting, the action is quickly learned. It begins with the rod tip held at shoulder level. Line has already been worked through the rod rings and lies ready to be picked up for the backcast. The rod point is lifted sharply taking the line upwards and back behind the angler. As the rod comes to the vertical position the lift is halted and the line extends behind. A deliberate pause is made at this point to allow the line to extend fully. When the line is felt to be pulling on the rod from behind, the forward cast is executed by swinging the tip forward and downward to turn the line over smoothly. The casting action ends at more or less the original position with the point of aim being slightly above the intended target. A high, smooth, smartly executed back cast ensures a good forward cast.

A hasty movement from the backward lift to the forward release will crack off the fly. A backcast that drops too low behind the caster, because the rod has been taken back too far, results in a bad and often tangled forward cast. Throughout the whole casting action the fly line is held in the left hand*. It is only released to shoot line at the end of the forward movement. When the line is felt to be pulling forward the left hand releases the line and the surplus is pulled through the rod rings.

*For right handed casters

float down over the top of a feeding trout, in a manner that does not cause suspicion. Any kind of drag imparted by the rod or drifting line will cause the fly to skid on the top, and the trout to retreat. It is not easy to learn to cast accurately, nor is it easy to 'cover' the fish without causing suspicion. However, trout tend to head upstream facing the food coming down with the current, and casting a dry fly involves an approach from *below* it. Standing actually behind the fish, and casting up in front of it so that only the fine leader holding the fly settles in the trout's window of vision, a good fly fisher can present his artificial fly so that it appears like any other natural insect coming down the stream. That's trout fishing at its best and, according to many experienced anglers, most satisfying.

I make no bones about it. I could not put the fly down accurately or delicately enough to fool those wise and wily trout, but fortunately all was not lost for me. I was still able to revert to

Leading casting expert Geoffrey Bucknall demonstrates the overhead cast in this photographic sequence.

the traditional wet fly approach.

The technique is entirely different, although the basic casting action with the rod is still the same. Line has to be extended from the rod rings and the fly has to be put in more or less the right place, but it does not necessarily have to drop like a piece of thistledown. The simple facts are that the dry-fly-fisher is casting upstream, to fish he can see, whereas the wet-fly-fisher is casting downstream and covering an area of water where trout are expected to be. An error in casting does little damage in the circumstances and, since the water is being searched for fish all the time, the novice stands more chance of success with a wet fly.

To fish a wet fly the line or, at least, the leader has to sink, and the cast is made down-and-across so that the fly comes round in the current, hopefully in front of a trout's nose.

Even wet fly casting requires practice, however, and it would be asking too much to go to a river and expect to catch trout without having at least a little experience. Ray told me, 'some tuition can be really beneficial, but many anglers are self-taught and most are agreed that practical experience is the important factor. Practice makes perfect, and you learn as you proceed, but it is important not to practise casting for too long at a time. Always take long rests in between sessions'.

Dry flies have to float on the water and in the main are tied with a hackle of buoyant neck feathers. Dry flies have to be dressed regularly with a floatant. False casting dries them out in the air ready for the next cast.

Wet flies are fished below the surface and are tied in a manner to make them sink. Hackle is sparse and "wings" are set back close to the hook shank.

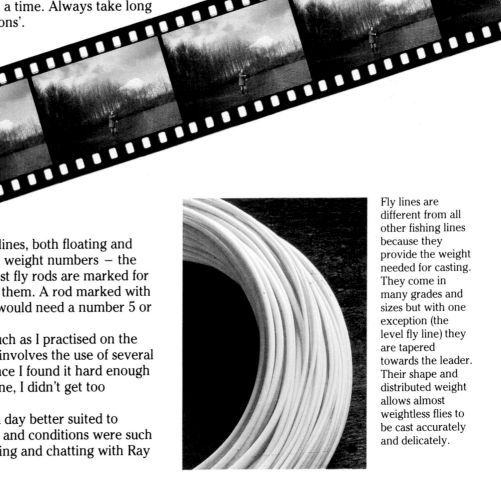

All of today's fly lines, both floating and sinking, are marked in weight numbers – the AFTM code – and most fly rods are marked for the line most suited to them. A rod marked with a 5 or 6, for instance, would need a number 5 or 6 fly line.

Wet fly fishing, such as I practised on the day in question, often involves the use of several flies in a 'team'; but since I found it hard enough to cope with just the one, I didn't get too ambitious.

It was, perhaps, a day better suited to talking than to fishing, and conditions were such that I found myself sitting and chatting with Ray from time to time.

Fly lines are different from all other fishing lines because they provide the weight needed for casting. They come in many grades and sizes but with one exception (the level fly line) they are tapered towards the leader. Their shape and distributed weight allows almost weightless flies to be cast accurately and delicately.

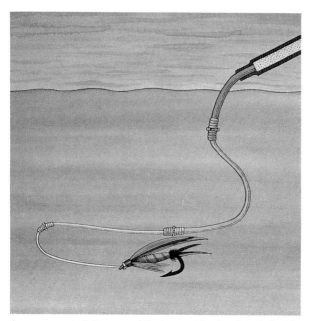

An exaggerated diagram of the tapered leader. It is tied with different thicknesses of monofilament and joins the thin end of the fly line to continue the natural taper. Most leaders are attached to the fly line with a needle or nail knot that allows them to be drawn through the rod rings. There are many leaders available today that are completely knotless and perfectly tapered by the manufacturers, but some fly fishers still prefer to make up their own.

We had some seven miles of river at our disposal and, since the hotel (on whose land we were fishing) restricts the number of anglers, we were unlikely to be disturbed.

The setting was glorious. We sat at the head of Miller's Pool and discussed the prospects. This is one pool where trout are sometimes fished for during the day time, with tiny flies. Sea trout are sought there later at night, with bigger flies and more substantial tackle. I had never fished for sea trout at night before and the prospects sounded exciting, but meanwhile I thought it was time to try to catch a brownie. I had made several attempts and failed. I had a look at the natural flies on the water and tried to match them but found it difficult with regard to wet fly fishing.

I knew, of course, that some experts tend to inspect the stomachs of any trout they catch by scooping with a marrow spoon. From this they are apparently able to tell what the other trout are taking but, as Ray said at the time, sometimes the contents are a bit unrecognisable.

Ray did not appear to be too enthusiastic about that particular procedure, and I wondered if he felt the same as some other anglers do about it. You see, it puzzles them. Ray explained, 'An angler may catch a trout and find that inside its stomach are lots of tiny nymphs, or whatever. That tells him what the trout he has just caught had been eating, but does it tell him what the others still not caught are eating? And how, if

these stomach contents are so important, did he manage to catch the trout in the first place on something entirely different?'

If, however, you can see insects coming down with the current, and are able to watch the trout taking them from the surface, it offers some suggestion as to the choice of fly. It is easier to 'match-the-hatch' when fishing with a dry fly. A simple selection of wet flies (in many cases not strictly representative of any particular natural insect) will usually bring about reasonable results.

I watched Ray fishing dry with one tiny floating black fly (a Connemara Black), and later fishing wet with a team of three. We discussed fly reels and their use: basically, a fly reel is only a spool to hold the fly line, it is not used to execute the cast.

We talked of the types of dry and wet flies that Ray uses, and the fly boxes he uses to protect them. Fly fishermen usually take great care of their flies, especially if they've tied their own. But with the river at an almost all-time low, the chances of catching trout during the day were remote and we both knew it. Nevertheless, it was an interesting experience to watch Ray casting with his split-cane rod, and to compare that with rods made of modern glass and carbon fibre. Today's carbon fibre wands are incredibly light and versatile, but in the hands of an expert there remains little to beat a craftsman-built split-cane rod. Ray had owned his for many years and was obviously very fond of it. The ease with which he used it indicated that he was familiar with its fine action. It was like an old friend to him and, although I was using an ultra-modern carbon fibre rod of very high quality, I doubt very much if I could have persuaded him to swap.

His action with a team of wet flies was simple. Cast across and down, let the flies swing round in the current, pick up the line, false cast, take a short step downstream, and cast again. That, I could see, was how to extract the most from a dour river and a difficult situation, but I knew deep down that our only real chance lay in fishing after dark.

There's a certain magic about fishing a sea trout river through the night. It is a situation entirely different from anything else I have ever experienced. Sea trout are very shy, very restless, and very easily scared. They respond to fishing after dark better than at any other time, and I still wonder how they manage to see the fly or lure in the darkness.

I am, however, in no doubt whatsoever that they have remarkable eyesight and I know that, in the interests of the camera work involved, we started fishing too early.

The purpose of the artificial fly is to present as natural-looking a bait as possible by imitating the natural insect or fly. Selection should be made at the time of fishing, by observing the natural flies which are being taken by the trout.

One of Britain's leading experts in the sea trout fishing field had this to say about night fishing, 'Wait until you are absolutely certain that it is too dark for the fish to see you, and then wait *another half an hour* before venturing to the water's edge.' Wise words!

We were more or less obliged to make an early start, of course, and as the light began to fail we tackled up and went our different ways. I moved downstream from Ray and fished a nice little run with no success. He chose to fish a lively bit of water upstream and cast into the shadows made by the overhanging trees. It was good thinking on his part. He could still see to cast, and it was better to fish an area where the darkness would appear to descend just that little bit more quickly.

I was left alone with my thoughts, and I remembered what others had said about sea trout fishing at night. It was all coming true. There was no loneliness, no apprehension, just a feeling of freedom and an awareness of the fact that nature never sleeps. At night time the water comes to life and, although the sounds of the night are magnified, they are friendly sounds.

1. Connemara Black
2. Partridge & Yellow
3. Snipe & Purple
4. Black & Peacock Spider
5. Alexandra
6. March Brown
7. Butcher
8. Royal Coachman
9. Coachman
10. Peter Ross

One of Ray King's favourite wet fly combinations for the Taw is the Partridge & Orange point fly, Snipe & Purple and Black Spider as first and second dropper.

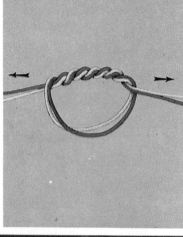

The water knot in more detail. This knot is used for a number of different rigs and in all branches of angling. Especially useful for tying droppers to main reel line.

A modern fly reel, lightweight and foolproof. All fly reels are basically simple centrepin reels with a drag or check incorporated. They serve no purpose with regard to the actual casting and serve merely as a reserve for spare line. Some anglers actually play a fighting trout or salmon by winding and releasing the reel handle to give line when necessary. Others simply let the line slip through their fingers and play the fish by handling.

An owl hooted close by, a fox spoke in the distance, the water chuckled as it rippled over the stony shallows, and even in these low conditions I could feel the slight pull around my feet.

A sea trout jumped clear of the surface and landed with a great splash back into the water but, although it startled me, it did not affect my casting rhythm as I worked my way down the pool. At any moment I expected to feel the decisive pull on my rod tip and an indication that the fly had been taken.

One of the great things about sea trout fishing after dark is that it can be precisely accurate.

By extending the right amount of line at the start, and holding that amount constant without putting any back on the reel (or taking any more off it) each cast will put the fly in the right place. The fly can only go to the extent of the line; it cannot be over extended and land on the far bank. The simple fly reel, with its check or drag mechanism, makes fishing in the dark much easier than it is with an open or closed-faced spinning reel.

Sea trout can be taken at various depths during the night and there are times when a big buzzy fly or lure, one that creates a wake on the surface, will be taken with sudden, almost unbelievable aggression. It happens mostly on very dark nights and, having seen sea trout leap in the darkness, I can well imagine the excitement a surface take would cause.

While I was alone with my thoughts and enjoying the summer night air, Ray was suddenly into a sea trout upstream from me, and I went to see what was happening.

It was not a very lively fish to begin with, and Ray seemed a bit disappointed because it wasn't leaping about all over the pool, but I could tell at once that it was a fish well worth catching. Ray, wisely, took his time and refused to be rushed. He said he had seen too many fish lost through impatience and, even if this one wasn't behaving in a spectacular fashion, it could still not be claimed until it was actually in the net.

The little split-cane rod bucked every so often, as the fish bored and sulked in the current. The reel screeched as the fish gained a few yards of line, and Ray kept the rod tip at a nice angle to absorb the sudden jerks. All the time he maintained a steady pressure, kept his cool, and gave a running commentary as to what was happening. 'It's no good trying to net the fish before they're really tired out and ready for the net. Now he's on his side, he's getting tired; get the net ready. He'll probably make a dive when I try to net him if I don't wait till he's tired out. He's not ready yet — he's going off again. Bring him round. Now he's coming in . . .', and so on.

It seemed like an age before Ray had him near to being beaten, and the fish that started off showing little fight at all was suddenly all over the pool and waking up to the fact that something was going wrong in its watery world.

Ray said, 'There's a lot more fight in him than I thought. I've got a fairly light leader, so I don't want to put too much pressure on, otherwise he'll be gone.' Then suddenly, 'Here he is – in the net. Right! A nice one!'

I had only been an onlooker, but I breathed a sigh of relief. I had been as anxious as the man with the rod, and perhaps more so. After all, he had done it so many times before!

Having seen one good fish caught, I moved off alone to try my luck again in the darkness. I became accustomed to the situation after a time and refrained from using a light near the water's edge. Using a small torch to change flies is about the only acceptable procedure on traditional sea trout rivers and, although I was obliged to tie on new flies from time to time (because I lost so many), I could see the sense of it all. Lights affect the ability to see in the dark. Complete rejection of lights allow the eyes to become familiarized with the surroundings, and fishing becomes comparatively easy.

And so I fished on through the night, wondering how Ray was doing, but enjoying every one of those stolen moments by the river. I *did* catch a sea trout. It was not large and there are many who might have referred to it as

immature, but to me it was a small silver-blue sea trout, fresh run from the sea. And, although it was not in the same class as Ray's fish, it gave me a great deal of pleasure. After all, I had caught it alone and unaided!

We made our way back to the hotel shortly after dawn with one good sea trout, one small sea trout (mine!), and two very fair brown trout to show for our efforts. I was tired, but the excitement of fishing under the stars, and the magic of a sea trout river at night, were still with me. It had been a super night. Not in terms of fish caught but in terms of sheer fishing pleasure, and an awareness of nature that only comes when the rest of the world is asleep.

I believe them all now when they say that sea trout fishing is the most exhilarating of all, and I hope the day will come when I can revisit the river, when a spate has brought up fresh fish from the sea.

As we weighed the catch and reminisced on the night hours just past, I reflected that this had been a trip I would always remember. We had not performed great deeds, but we had enjoyed our fishing, and had something to show for our efforts.

'It matters not who won or lost, it's how you played the game,' I quoted. I've always felt that way. On reflection, I might just as easily have quoted Dame Juliana Berners who is reputed to have said, in 1496, that 'there is more to fishing than catching fish'. She, too, must have been a sea trout fisher!

Sea trout flies are generally larger versions of traditional wet flies. Silver and blue are very popular colours for night fishing. Hook sizes usually range from 10 to 6.

Reservoir Trout Fishing

An excellent day's catch, both Jack and Bob Church look well pleased with themselves. Bob Church, captor of a 31½ lb (14 kg) limit at Grafham Water, and a 16¾ lb (7.5 kg) rainbow from Avington, remains one of Britain's best known angling personalities.

When I was making my way up to Rutland Water, to fish with Bob Church, I had in mind the prospect of an exciting day's fishing, because Rutland had a reputation for brown and some large rainbow trout.

I reflected, as I drove along, on the way trout fishing in Britain has developed over the past 15 years. Once it was a sport practised only by the privileged and wealthy few; now trout fishing is available to anyone with a fly rod and a day to spare. Rutland Water is but one of the many reservoirs offering trout fishing on a day ticket basis. It is, however, one of the latest and one of the largest man-made reservoirs in Europe.

I knew, of course, that as a stranger and comparative novice, I could not hope to go to that vast expanse of water and drop on fish at once. Without professional guidance and advice from the staff who know the ropes, I would be hopelessly lost. That's why I played it smart. If you want to find out about still-water trout you go to the expert, and Bob Church is about the best there is.

It was a beautiful day. The weather was perfect when Bob and I met to discuss prospects and, although I was almost desperate to get started, I couldn't help drooling for a while over his selection of flies. Many of them simply could not be regarded as flies at all. They were lures, pure and simple, dressed to represent small fish. One in particular, a white monstrosity with a wagging tail, looked fit to hold a shark, but Bob explained that it was a bit of a specialist lure for fishing very deep. He had many other attractor-type lures, buoyant flies, wet flies, nymphs and pukka dry flies. We were, without doubt, ready for anything that happened to come our way, and his specialist tackle did not end there. Bob had even brought along his own anchor, since he believed it to be better than the one supplied. Not, he hastened to assure me, that there was any risk involved in using the boats on Rutland! Big winds would get up occasionally, of course, but the boats were stable, and in the event of a breakdown white flares were on board to attract

41

attention. Should an angler be taken ill, a red flare would bring help out at once. The water was always under surveillance, he said, and the emphasis at all times was upon safety. In really rough conditions, boats were confined to shore for obvious reasons.

Trout fishing on big still-waters differs in so many respects from other branches of the sport, that it really demands a specialist approach if consistent results are to be maintained. There are three basic types of fishing which may be listed as lure fishing, drifting in traditional loch style, and nymph fishing; and, of course, occasionally there comes the opportunity to fish with dry flies, like big sedge moths on the surface.

The style of fishing being practised more or less decides the kind of line required. Obviously, to fish on or very close to the surface, a floating line is indicated. To fish a lure deep, a fast sinking line would probably be the number one choice. Where long casting is necessary a shooting head, that is to say about 10 yd (9 m) of tapered fly line attached to a much thinner length of braided or monofilament backing, allows distance to be covered more easily than with a full fly-line.

Those facts are fairly easy to absorb, but the whole business may become over-complicated when slow sinking lines, sink tip lines, medium sinkers and even lead-cored lines have to be

Fly lines and their various uses.
Top to Bottom: Floating flyline
                             Floating shooting head
                             Sink-tip fly line
                             Slow sinker
                             Medium sinker
                             Fast sinker
                             Lead cored line.
All have their uses in still-water fly fishing but traditional river trout fishing does not call for such extremes.

Double Taper
The traditional shape of line; fine tips at each end; thick belly in the middle. Reversible for longer wear. Usually 30 yd (28 m).
Weight Forward
Casting weight is compressed into the head of the line to give a projectile effect in the air for distance casting.
Shooting Head
Exaggerated form of weight-forward line, whereby a short length of 30 ft (25 m) heavy line is spliced to a very fine shooting line. Used for distance casting from reservoir banks.

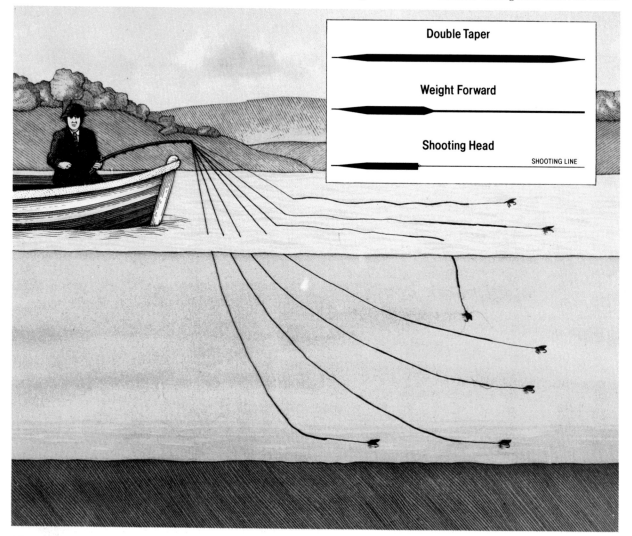

Double Taper

Weight Forward

Shooting Head

SHOOTING LINE

considered. Then, of course, there are permutations of all the basic methods to deal with the really tricky situations. It is small wonder that some of the specialist reservoir anglers go equipped with a minimum of six fly reels, all holding something different in the way of lines or shooting heads.

As we began making our first tentative casts, I marvelled on the fact that Rutland's brown trout commonly top the 4 lb (1.8 kg) mark. It's not so long ago that any fly-caught trout weighing 4 lb (1.8 kg) or over was regarded as an unusual angling feat. A bottle of sherry could, at one time, be claimed by any fly fisher who could offer proof of such a fish. Today, rainbow trout of twice that weight are not particularly rare!

I cast my Black Chenille lure, and retrieved it at odd speeds to try to feel out the situation. I felt a few plucks here and there, but couldn't connect at all. I wondered if I was allowing it to sink long enough, or if I was retrieving it too quickly or too slowly. Bob thought that my hook size might be a bit on the large side, and that I should step down from a 6 to an 8, so he dug one out of his box for me. Same pattern, different size. I still experienced plucks, but no connections.

It was comfortable fishing for us both. The boat rudder was rigged to let us drift bow

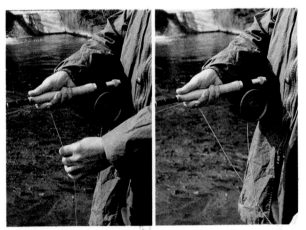

Flies, lures and nymphs may be made to appear alive and moving naturally by stripping in line after casting. This is usually referred to as the retrieve and is seldom carried out by using the reel. Instead, movement is imparted by drawing in by hand and the speed and action of the fly is related to the angler's drawing in of the line. Lures are often stripped in at high speed with long fast pulls. Nymphs are often retrieved an inch at a time — very slowly.

forward, instead of broadside, and Bob and I covered a great deal of water without hindering each other's casting. I changed flies again — still without response.

Suddenly Bob was into a fish. A rainbow he thought — and so it turned out to be. It had taken a small Squirrel & Silver lure, fished fast and close to the surface. I did the honours, netted Bob's fish, and returned to my casting. It was not a monster by any means, but a nice silver specimen weighing about 1½ lb (0.6 kg). I reflected at the time that it would be a prime eating fish, and suddenly I was into a fish myself. It, too, was a rainbow, small but full of steam. It had taken a small black and silver fly called the Ace of Spades. Its size disappointed me a little, but we decided to retain it just in case. After all, a fish in the boat is worth more than two in the water!

There are many anglers who believe in returning unsuitable fish to the water. They maintain that they wish only to keep the best, and that returning the unwanted does no harm. Bob thinks, as I do, that once a trout has been hooked and subjected to a very exhausting experience on the end of a line, it might as well be retained. Many, if not most, of the trout returned in those circumstances are unlikely to survive.

It became obvious, after two more fish had come to net, that fishing fast, using small lures

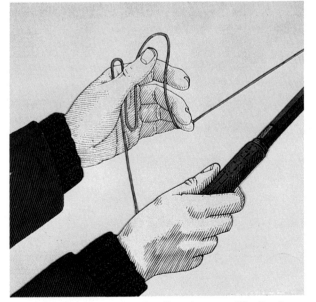

The figure-of-eight retrieve is self-explanatory. The line is bunched by figure-of-eight movements in the left hand and the action of the fly is decided by the speed and timing of the retrieve.

Rainbow trout

Introduced from America in the last century for releasing into rivers and lakes. Stocked throughout Britain. A handsome fish, with darkish green back, a magenta flash on the flanks, lightening to a silvery-white belly. Takes fly freely and fights with verve, leaping high in the air when hooked. A shoal fish and a great roamer, preferring to spend much time near the surface.

(Left) **1.** Ace of Spades, **2.** Black Chenille, **3.** Alexandra, **4.** Sweeney Todd, **5.** Appetiser, **6.** Whiskey Fly, **7.** Mickey Finn, **8.** Sweeney Todd, **9.** Orange Polystickle, **10.** Squirrel & Yellow, **11.** Goldie, **12.** Tandem Silver & White, **13.** Jack Frost, **14.** Green Polystickle, **15.** Muddler Minnow.

with plenty of flash on the retrieve, was the right tactic. Rainbows are aggressive fish, and we were teasing them into striking rather than tempting them to feed. On another day, or in colder conditions, we may have found a slow retrieve to be the answer; or we might have found it necessary to inch small nymphs along, close to the bottom, to represent natural food. The options are wide open, but all of them are interesting.

Suddenly, there we were, both into a fish at the same time and, since I had been retrieving quite slowly at the time, the fast retrieve theory went overboard! It seemed not to matter much what the lure or the rate of retrieve happened to be. What we had to do was find the fish and leave the rest to them!

We whooped and hollered a bit until both those fish were on board. I remember that we both cussed a bit, too, from time to time, but then it was one of those days!

I learnt a lot from Bob. How to play a fish by letting line slide through my fingers, instead of trying to get it all back on the reel. With the size of fish we were catching it didn't really matter too much, anyway, but Bob explained, 'There are times when a big fish can tear off at such a pace that the reel cannot give line quickly enough. The result, of course, is a broken leader and a lost fish.'

Halfway through the morning we were approaching half our legal limit, each. The personal limit at Rutland is eight fish but it is possible, in the event that a limit comes quickly, to purchase another ticket and carry on fishing; and when it began to appear that we might limit out by lunchtime, I threatened to do just that, so good was the sport on that day.

We didn't tire of catching fish, nor did they 'go off' at all. However, for the sake of variety, Bob and I decided to change tactics and try a traditional loch style drift on another part of the reservoir, after lunch.

It's a delightful way of catching trout, using the breeze to move the boat. A lot of water is covered and each short cast with the wind behind puts the fly, or flies, into fresh territory. If a fish is missed, there's no going back. A second or two later it has been left behind the drifting boat. A drogue can be used, to slow down the boat's passage in the wind.

In Scotland, on the bigger lochs where this method probably originated, a team of flies is used. Sometimes as many as four flies are presented on droppers, but most anglers find three enough to handle comfortably. I settled for two!

The technique is simple enough. Once the boat is drifting nicely, broadside on, short casts are made forward, and the flies are brought back with a quick stripping-and-lifting action to make them skip along the surface. The cast is fished out within a few seconds and, as the boat moves on, a fresh cast covers a new spot.

So our day continued. Success and failure, hits and misses, but never a dull moment. During breaks in the proceedings we discussed tackle and techniques and I began once again to drool over Bob's fly box. He picked out a selection of flies and lures that he felt would suit most situations, and I accepted graciously a Muddler Minnow, a Black Chenille, a Sweeney Todd, a Whiskey Fly, an Appetiser and a Jack Frost. There is very little similarity among any of them, but even I knew their reputations as fish killers.

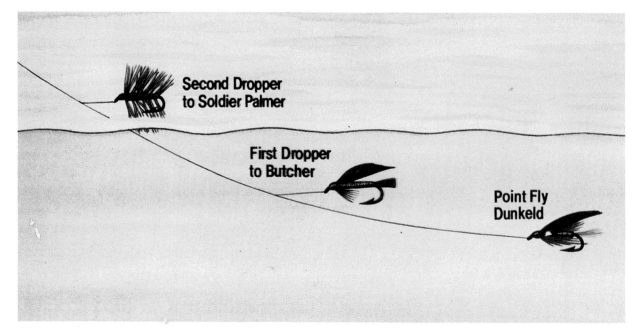

Second Dropper
to Soldier Palmer

First Dropper
to Butcher

Point Fly
Dunkeld

When using more than one wet fly (usually a team of three) on a leader it is customary to tie all but the point fly to a dropper. This is a short piece of nylon monofilament tied to the main leader using a water-knot. The fly on the first dropper above the point fishes slightly shallower and the fly on the second dropper is often tied in a buzzy Palmer fashion to fish on or very close to the surface. In many cases it may be used as a floating indicator to detect rises to the other flies. In the event that it suddenly disappears under the surface, it may be assumed that one of the other flies has been taken.

A drogue is a device used to slow down a boat drifting naturally on a still water. It may be made of net, canvas or plastic, and it can be attached at different points to suit conditions. It simply holds the boat steady against the pull of the wind and allows the drift to proceed slowly while the area is being searched. Drogues are essential, especially in windy conditions, for traditional loch-style fishing.

I'm not into the entomology side of trout fishing, but do tie up a few lure flies of my own, so I know the names of a good many of them. I tried to trip Bob up once by challenging him to name those I picked out from his box, but I should have known better. He knew them all by heart, and even the reasons for most of their given names.

Still hoping for a bigger fish, still thinking I might connect with one of the famous brown trout, I carried on fishing with my two flies on the drift. It's a pleasant way of fishing, not in any way tiring, and I enjoyed seeing the flies skipping along the top.

Suddenly I was into something a little better than I had handled previously. It took on the top, quite spectacularly from my point of view, and Bob accused me (as he had been doing all day) of taking too long to subdue it. He reckoned I had value for money with every fish I caught, but I like to take my time about landing my fish. I have seen fish lost through careless handling and trying to get them in the net too quickly.

It was Bob who took the best fish of the day — you didn't expect anything else, did you? I didn't take its exact weight, but I reckon it was about twice as big as anything we'd caught previously. Then it was my turn to suggest that Bob was hanging things out a bit himself! Great fun, good company, and a super day's fishing.

We went back to the lodge with a boat limit of sixteen fish. Bob had taken nine and I had given him a fair run with my seven. They weighed together about 21 lb (9.5 kg), and were all in fine condition.

In the circumstances, we had done very well. It had been a bright July day, the water had been warming up, and the fish had not been too easy to locate. In the main, the Squirrel & Silver had proved to be our best pattern for the day, but I confess that taking fish near the surface on the drift was the exercise that really appealed to me. There is something rather special about taking 'em on top.

I tried to claim that, although Bob beat me in numbers, I had caught the biggest fish and that my seven weighed more than his nine, but somehow I doubt if anyone believed me!

Even so, I had never been associated with a double limit (a day's single limit at Rutland is 8 trout) anywhere before, and I have to admit that it did my confidence a power of good. But enough was enough and we quit while we were winning. No one could have enjoyed a day more than I enjoyed that one.

I hope Bob enjoyed it as much as I did, and deep down I feel sure he did.

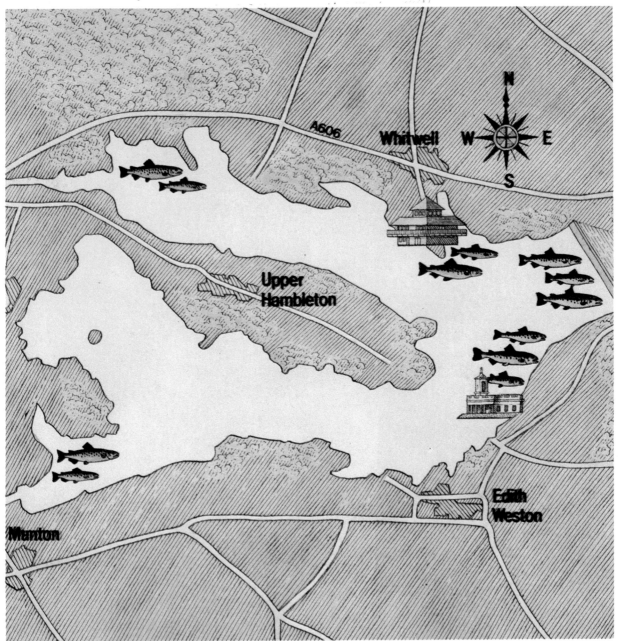

Rutland Water, one of Britain's largest and most modern trout reservoirs, is noted for its quality brown trout as well as its prolific rainbows. It is made up of two long arms of water fed by two natural streams. Trout are fairly evenly distributed, though there are a few barren areas. It is possible to drift both arms in certain conditions and this method, covering as it does a great area of water, eventually puts the angler among the fish.

In the early part of the season the dam end seems to offer the best chances. The Normanton Church area and the expanse in front of the lodge are popular early season spots. Later the arms begin to fish well and many big fish are caught still later in the shallows at the end of each arm. Information is readily given regarding conditions by a staff of enthusiastic professionals and safety precautions are of the highest order. Rutland Water offers fly fishing to everyone on a day ticket basis. It offers every kind of still-water trout fishing, from boat and bank.

Salmon Fishing

Ever since I caught my first salmon on the river Eden, some years ago, I've always wanted to tie into a big Scottish salmon from a river like the beautiful Tay. I can still remember the excitement of that first fish, and the panic of it all. I'm pretty sure I made some mistakes, but I got it on the bank somehow or other, and there's no doubt at all that it whetted my appetite for more.

So, when the opportunity came to fish the river Tay at Dunkeld, with an expert like Jess Miller, I jumped at it. I naturally wanted to fish, *and* I wanted to catch a salmon, but I also wanted to see an expert salmon angler at work. Jess has been on the river since he was seven years old – he should know a thing or two!

There are a number of ways of fishing for salmon, but the two basic methods are spinning and fly fishing. Of the two, fly fishing is the more artistic and demands more skill; in the right hands, and in the right conditions, the fly rod is a powerful tool; but overall the spinning rod probably takes more fish over a long period.

I watched Jess executing beautiful casts with his double-handed carbon-fibre rod. Poetry in motion I called it, but we both knew that fly fishing chances were slim. He tried a big Thunder and Lightning fly just on the off-chance, and I had a short spell with a lighter, 10½ ft (3.2 m) single-handed fly rod, and a smaller fly (a Dunkeld) just for the experience. I used a floating line and made short casts. I don't handle a big fly rod too well, and I'm not strictly into the double-haul cast yet.

Jess's selection of flies was fascinating, many of which were unknown to me. The larger tube flies – flies actually tied on to lead or plastic tubes – were all new to me. But the river was too high for effective fly fishing, so we had to reluctantly put them away and put up suitable spinning rods. After a few months of drought, heavy rains had made the river dirty and brown, but there was some consolation in the fact that it had brought plenty of fish up into the pools.

We needed something big and heavy to get down deep in the edge of the current. We also needed something that would flash and be visible in the murk and, while there were plenty of

Jess Miller and Jack discuss Jess's collection of spinners.

options open, including the very popular Devon minnow in its many different colours and sizes, we eventually opted for spoons. Devons, smaller spoons, prawns, shrimps, worms and of course, flies of all sizes, would come into their own when the water became conditioned later, but for the day in question spoons – fished deep – offered our best chance.

On Jess's advice I used a line of 20 lb (9 kg) breaking strain and chose, as my lure, a streamlined copper spoon. It was heavy, but still required extra weight to get it down to the fish, and I added this in the shape of a big spiral lead which I attached to the trace above the swivel, called a Jardine.

The water above us was deep and turbulent. It went down to 40 ft (12m) or so, but shallowed to 20 ft (6m) just in front of us. The fish, said Jess, were lying between our bank and the middle of the river, in the somewhat quieter water. I could see at once, and knew from past experience, that I had to cast up and across, allowing the spoon to swing round in the current. I also knew that I had to keep in touch with it, by winding slowly as it came back round to my bank.

The important factor was to let it sink and work slow and deep. Casting slightly upstream gave it time to sink before the current took charge and, apart from maintaining contact with the reel, I more or less let the tackle fish for itself with each cast. I could feel the spoon working at the end of the taut line, and could see it flashing below the surface as it reached the end of the retrieve.

There's a certain rhythm involved in fishing for salmon, and somehow it's important to maintain this, steadily, all the time. Cast, retrieve, move down, cast, retrieve, and so on. At any moment the sheer magic of that tug on the rod top may come, and it's then important to remain composed.

In the circumstances I felt sure, and Jess confirmed, that a taking salmon would mean business. If it came for the spoon, or lure, it would do so because it intended to nail it! A salmon hits a lure with such speed and determination that it literally hooks itself. A frantic strike at this stage could well snatch the hook from its mouth and a golden chance could be lost. I steeled myself into remembering this as I continued the rhythmic process, and weighed up the prospects.

The fish at this time of year could be 'stale'. That's to say they could have been in the river for a long time, or they could be freshly run from the sea because of the high water conditions.

A three-piece, carbon-fibre, double-handed fly rod as used for salmon fishing. The fly reel fitting is positioned high up the handle to allow for the left-hand grip below.

Tube flies are used as alternatives to the larger single-hooked salmon flies. They are tied on small tubes which are slid over the leader which is then tied to an appropriate treble hook. Some tubes are leaded to make them fish deeper.

The Green Highlander is a famous Scottish Highland salmon fly.

The popular Dunkeld salmon fly, named after the town in Scotland.

The famous Black Doctor salmon fly has been killing salmon since the 1890s and is just one of the very successful 'Doctor' flies. Especially recommended when there is colour in the water.

High water brings in new fish from the sea, and encourages those already in the river to move upstream towards their spawning beds. They may spawn at any time during November and December, and it is all over by the time the season opens, on January 15th. Many do not recover from spawning, but a small percentage (Jess reckons between 2 and 10 per cent) manage to return to sea for the second time. What, I wondered, were the chances of them returning to the river yet again in a few years time? In the event that they did, they would have to be in the 30-40 lb (13.5-18.0 kg) class. Some fish!

An incredible fish, the salmon. Its life cycle is one that always intrigues me, and its fight against all the odds to return to the river of its birth has always commanded my respect and admiration. Its whole life is beset by obstacles from start to finish, but the desire to reproduce is so fierce that it never ceases in its attempt to reach its goal.

It begins life as an egg on the spawning redds, hatches into an alevin and survives for some weeks on the yolk sac still attached to its body. Soon it grows and becomes known as a parr, at which stage it begins to forage for itself. Even at this stage it is vulnerable to predators of many kinds. At two years old it develops to the smolt stage, and migrates to the open sea where it becomes somewhat of a mystery.

It grows quickly, feeding on the rich marine life, and on occasions returns to the river within a year. A salmon of this calibre weighing perhaps 4 or 5 lb (1.8 or 2.3 kg) is known as a grilse.

Most of those that make it back as adults do so after two or more years and, whatever their age, they then become the angler's legitimate quarry.

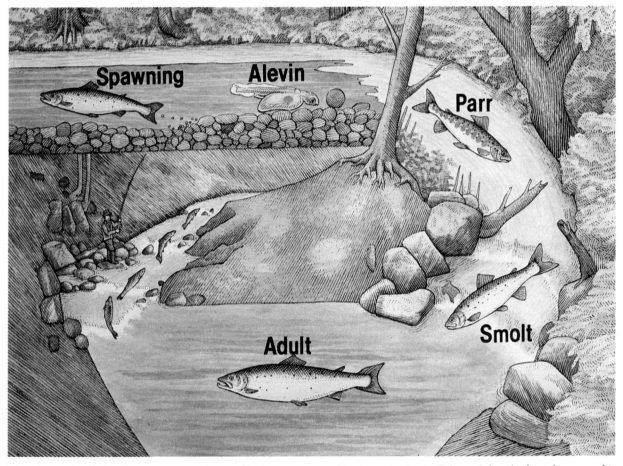

The salmon starts life as an egg on the redds — a shallow scooped-out hole in the gravel — during the winter months. It hatches into an alevin in about three months and develops to the parr stage some time later. At this stage it begins to forage for itself, having exhausted the contents of its earlier yolk sac. In slightly less than two years it becomes a smolt with an urge to go to sea, and this it does as a mere 6 in (150 mm) long infant.
In the sea it grows quickly by feeding on the rich marine life, and it may grow to 20-30 lb (9-13 kg) before returning to the river of its birth. Fish much heavier have been caught and it is generally thought that the very big ones have returned for the second time. Of those smolts that make their way to sea, a few return after only a year or a little more. They have reached a weight of 4-6 lb (2-3 kg) in their brief period in salt water and are referred to as grilse. A spawned-out adult salmon making its way back to sea for the second time is known as a kelt. Such fish are pitiful creatures and it is illegal to retain them. Experienced salmon fishermen always return them to the water.

The amazing aspect of fishing for salmon, however, is that once back in fresh water, the fish stops feeding. It uses up its natural body fats and survives the whole course on that alone, so why does it then take a fly, or a spoon, prawn, worm, or whatever? If we tell the truth, we don't know. Some say a salmon snatches at a passing lure out of anger or irritation. Others say that, although it does not feed in the true sense of the word, it strikes at what looks like food through force of habit. For years it has foraged at sea and no doubt snapped at passing titbits, too. It is understandable that it should do so instinctively in fresh water. This may help to explain why 'stale' fish tend to be more difficult to catch than those that are fresh run.

My thoughts wandered on, but I maintained my rhythm. The day was warm and I revelled in the atmosphere. It seemed that I became lost in what I was doing. I seemed to blend with the beautiful surrounding countryside and felt I had become a part of it.

A sudden stop, almost a jerk on the rod tip, brought me to my senses and I thought that, at last, Lady Luck had chosen to smile on me. But it was not to be. This was no fish, but the bottom, pure and simple. I pulled the tackle free and carried on fishing.

Jess was using a multiplying reel which, though more difficult to use, is much more versatile than the closed face reel of the type I was using, and at one stage I felt the urge to try a few casts with his outfit. I knew it would take me some time to get the hang of it, and I made a tentative short cast to 'feel' it out.

Once again I experienced the sudden stop, the jerk on the rod tip; and I thought, 'Damn, I'm caught on the bottom again!' I pulled to regain the tackle and, at that moment, the issue became somewhat confused. The bottom to which I was attached began to move, and I all but hit the panic button. Unbelievably, and against all the odds, I was suddenly into a fish; and it felt like a good one!

I'd wanted to try the multiplier, but now that I was attached to a salmon I wished I had my own outfit. At least I was familiar with that, and knew how to apply pressure and adjust the clutch. Now here I was with a strange rod, an even stranger reel, and a salmon trying to put distance between us. Not the best of situations, but I was bubbling with excitement while at the same time scared half to death that we were going to part company. I began to wish I hadn't remarked earlier that I'd be happy to have a fish

Devon minnows are true salmon spinning baits. They are made from many different materials including wood, plastic and metal. Buoyant Devons made of balsa and other woods are particularly useful in snaggy conditions.

Blades such as Mepps or Jenson have a blade, shaped like a small flat spoon, which spins rapidly around a central bar. They do not kink line and can be fluttered in the water. Gold, copper, silver and black are popular.

Toby spoons with their peculiar shapes and fin projections are favourites with salmon anglers all over the world. They come in many colours and sizes.

The multiplier reel holds heavy breaking strain line, and has a free revolving drum and a level wind mechanism. The star drag clutch allows a strong fish to take line and prevents breakage.

The side cast. Where the situation does not allow for a traditional overhead cast, the side cast is used as an alternative. The same procedure is used but the whole cast is carried out with the rod held horizontally. The pause is made when the rod is at the extent of its back cast as before, and the timing of the forward cast is exactly the same as that applied to the overhead cast. It is simply the same cast on a different plane and is extremely useful when trees and background obstructions prevent the traditional overhead cast. Leading casting expert Geoffrey Bucknall demonstrates.

on, and lose it. I knew then that I hadn't meant what I'd said!

The multiplier fortunately, but understandably since it had just been in the hands of an expert, had its clutch set correctly and, with some sound advice from Jess, I began pumping and winding, trying to gain line. When the fish made off on one of its mad rushes I simply let it go, and the clutch allowed line to come off the spool. Theoretically there was no chance of the line being broken, but I knew, even from limited experience, that strange things happen in practice. I could feel the surges of power beneath my thumb as the fish bored deeply a short way out; and controlled its rushes by clamping my thumb on the spool, and pumping in line whenever I saw the chance. In these circumstances winding the reel handle against a pulling fish is largely a waste of time. The fish pulls line off the spool as fast as you try to put it back on, and the result is stalemate. It's not good practice. Jess advised, 'The correct procedure is to lower the rod tip, winding in the slack line at the same time, then clamping the thumb on the reel spool to prevent any more line from being taken. 'Pump' or lift the rod up to gain the slack line, and the advantage. In the event of a sudden surge from the fish, you simply lift up the thumb and let it have its head.'

I half expected the fish to tear off downstream and use the current to its advantage, but luck was with me. It made many short controllable runs, but stayed strictly within the confines of the big pool. While I played the fish, Jess stood by, quietly offering advice and explaining that some salmon can travel up to 30 miles (48 km) in a day, and become very tired. The one I was attached to seemed to be far from tired!

Remembering, suddenly, that this was being filmed, I thought it would perhaps make sense if I brought the fish nearer the surface. Up until now it had not shown, and I realised that *I* wanted to see it as well as those who would view it later!

'Put your thumb on the drum and lift him up. He's getting tired now,' said Jess.

He didn't feel very tired to me, but I did as I was told and there he was. At least here was proof that a salmon existed and that it was on the end of *my* line.

After about fifteen minutes of give and take, I could tell that the fish was beginning to tire and, although I refused to admit it at the time, I began to realise that I was tired, too.

What if it made a mad rush when we came to the crucial moment of landing it by hand?

It sometimes happens, Jess told me, 'A lot of salmon escape when they appear to be completely beaten.' I swore there and then that I'd dive in and haul it out if such a thing happened to me!

It took one or two attempts to get it ashore but, following Jess's instructions, I maintained a steady pressure without forcing the issue. Once it made off to the middle of the river and gave me a mild heart attack, but eventually the hand-grip slid home around the tail and the fish was on the bank!

I collapsed in a heap and heaved a sigh of relief. Only those who have experienced it can appreciate the feeling.

Jess tapped the salmon on the head with a 'priest' to dispatch it. I noticed a nervous twitch in the body and decided that, dispatched or not,

it was too near the water's edge for my liking! After all I'd gone through, I was not about to lose my prize through carelessness! I hauled it a yard or two higher up the bank.

The absence of a hook, or kype, on the lower jaw identified it as a female fish in fine condition. Its weight was over 18 lb (8 kg) and there had never been any doubts regarding the hook-hold. Two points of the treble hook were firmly embedded, and served to bear out Jess's predictions that these fish do indeed hook themselves.

I was as proud as a peacock. Jess was obviously delighted and, as we held up the fish for all to see, I marked the whole event down as one of the highlights of my angling life.

Jess demonstrates the pumping action, while Jack controls the still-fighting salmon.

A prize to remember! Against all the odds, Jack holds his pride and joy, an 18 lb (8 kg) female salmon.

Jack's Angling Code

Fishing needs all the friends it can get at the moment. There are too many people ready to attack our great sport. So why give them any ammunition? If we all follow a code of conduct on the riverbank then at least we know that our own house is in order.

It should go without saying that all litter should be taken home, and not strewn along the bank like a refuse tip. You can now be banned from many waters for leaving litter. And that rule is not before time. Look at a peg after anglers like Ken Giles or Dick Clegg have been fishing. And all you'll see is some dropped groundbait, or loose maggots. Everything else goes home with them. The wild birds, particularly in cold weather, are always grateful for any titbits that are left.

This brings me nicely to the next point – nylon line. Nothing brings angling more into disrepute than a member of the public finding a wild bird ensnared in discarded line. And it's all so totally unnecessary. Any length of loose nylon should be either burnt on the spot, or carefully coiled together and taken home. The same applies to lead shot, whether loose or on the line. We've taken quite enough stick from naturalists over swan deaths from lead-shot poisoning. Even if we aren't to blame, don't give them any chance to point the finger in our direction. Take your shot home. It's soft enough to use again.

You'll want a licence before you go fishing. If you try to get away without one, it's odds on that a bailiff will appear. And he won't be impressed by stories that you didn't know one was needed. The same applies to day tickets, or club books. All waters belong to someone, even if there's no sign saying so.

When you're on the bank, never put your basket or seat too close to someone else already fishing. Give them at least 25 yd (23 m) of bank, where possible. And they may not appreciate the latest cricket score, or pop tunes, blared at them from a portable radio. Many waters ban these, along with dogs. Always check first on the back of your ticket. It will save some embarrassing moments later when you're asked to leave.

Disturb the bank as little as possible. You may need to bend a few reeds, but don't attempt the demolition of the river-bank in your efforts to create a swim.

Trout fishing calls for a whole new set of rules. You'll find most of them pinned up in big letters on the fishery lodge door. Disobey them at your peril. But there are certain unwritten rules that the newcomer should be aware of. The first is never approach too close to another fly-fisher, whether from the boat or bank. He may not say anything because he's too polite, but he'll certainly be thinking it. And if you are drifting the boat, make sure that you don't drift down on top of a boat where anglers are fishing at anchor. When you're under motor always give any other boats a wide berth, especially in shallow water. Then you should really cut your engine and get out the oars.

We've covered sea wreck fishing in this book, so it's probably worth mentioning a few unwritten rules of the sea. Always go afloat well prepared with waterproofs, warm clothing and non-slip footwear. That doesn't mean studded boots. And make sure you have sufficient leads, hooks, beads and swivels with you. You're going to lose a few, and you don't want to have to beg them from other people. Take a sharp filleting knife, too, so that you can do your share of cutting baits and gutting the catch. That's one of the attractions of boat fishing. Everyone mucks in together, and by the end of the trip even strangers are the best of friends.

Readers may like to know that Collins also publishes the *Encyclopedia of Fishing in Britain and Ireland,* edited by Michael Prichard, and described by Angling Times as "a must for every angler".
The *Encyclopedia* has contributions from Allen Edwards, Ivan Marks, Michael Prichard, John Holden and Reg Righyni. It also features Dr Dietrich Burkel's famous fish species illustrations (a few of which appear in this book in smaller size). The *Encyclopedia* has 256 pages, hundreds of colour pictures, and is priced at only £8.95.

WATER AUTHORITIES

All area Water Authorities are generally responsible for fisheries in their region, organising licensing, pollution control and investigation, stocking and bailiffing.

Anglian Water Authority
Ambury House, Huntingdon, Cambs.

North West Water Authority
Dawson House, Liverpool Road, Great Sankey, Warrington, Cheshire.

Northumbrian Water Authority
Northumbria House, Regent Centre, Gosforth, Newcastle upon Tyne NE3 3PX.

Severn Trent Water Authority
Abelson House, 2297 Coventry Rd., Sheldon, Birmingham B26 3PU.

South West Water Authority
3-5 Barnfield Rd., Exeter, Devon.

Southern Water Authority
Guild Bourne House, Chatsworth Rd., Worthing, Sussex BN11 1LD.

Thames Water Authority
New River Head, Rosebery Ave., London EC1R 4TP.

Welsh Water Authority
Cambrian Way, Brecon, Powys LD3 7HP.

Wessex Water Authority
Wessex House, Passage St., Bristol, Avon BS2 0JQ.

Yorkshire Water Authority
West Riding House, 67 Albion St., Leeds LS1 5AA.

No Water Authority licence is needed to fish in Scotland.

MAJOR ORGANISATIONS

Anglers' Co-operative Association
Midland Bank Chambers, Westgate, Grantham, Lincs. NH31 6LE.

Angling Foundation
D. Orton, The Limes, Alvechurch, Worcs.

Angling Trade Association
7 Swallow St., London W1R 7HD.

Association of Professional Game Angling Instructors
26 Linghill, Newby, Scarborough, N. Yorks.

Association of Sea Fisheries Committees of England & Wales
11 Clive Ave., Lytham St. Annes, Lancs. FY8 2RU.

The Atlantic Salmon Trust Ltd.
14 Downing St., Farnham, Surrey.

Birmingham Anglers Association
100 Icknield Port Rd., Rotton Park, Birmingham B16 0AP.

British Field Sports Society
59 Kennington Rd., London SE1 7PZ.

Scottish Branch
Glenmore Lodge, Moffat, Dumfries & Galloway, Scotland.

Welsh Branch
Woodpiece, Llandewi, Llandrindod Wells, Powys, Wales.

British Light Tackle Club
10 Southcote Rd., Tufnell Park, London N19 5BJ.

British Record (Rod-caught) Fish Committee
c/o National Anglers Council
5 Cowgate, Peterborough, Cambs.

British Tourist Authority
64-65 St. James's St., London SW1A 1NF

British Waterways Board
Willow Grange, Church Rd., Watford,
Herts. WD1 3QA.

Confederation of English Fly Fishers
Ferosa, Whitsbury, Fordingbridge, Hants.

Endeavour Deep Sea Group
Schooners Landing, Aberystwyth, Dyfed, Wales.

European Federation of Sea Anglers
11 Park Circus, Ayr, Scotland KA7 2DJ.

International Fly Fishing Association
P.O. Box 84, 51 Meadowside, Dundee DD1 5PQ.

London Anglers Association
183 Hoe St., Walthamstow, London E17

National Anglers Council
5 Cowgate, Peterborough, Cambs.

National Federation of Anglers
Halliday House, 2 Wilson St., Derby DE1 1PG.

National Federation of Charter Skippers
9 Dunstall Ave., Burgess Hill, Sussex RH15 8PJ.

The National Federation of Sea Anglers
26 Downsview Crescent, Uckfield TN22 1UB.

Salmon & Trout Association
Fishmongers' Hall, London Bridge,
London EC4R 9EL.

Scottish Anglers Association
117 Hanover St., Edinburgh, Scotland EH2 1DJ.

The Scottish National Angling Clubs'
Association
P.O. Box 84, 51 Meadowside, Dundee DD1 5PQ.

Scottish Salmon Angling Federation
c/o 18 Abercromby Place, Edinburgh 3.

Sea Angling Liaison Committee of Great
Britain and Ireland
5 Cowgate, Peterborough, Cambs.

Sports Council
16 Upper Woburn Place, London WC1H 0QP.

Welsh Anglers Council
87 Shirley Drive, Heolgerrig, Merthyr Tydfil,
Mid Glam.

Welsh Federation of Coarse Anglers
16 Whiterock Close, Graigwen, Pontypridd,
Mid Glam.

Welsh Federation of Sea Anglers
34 Coveny St., Splott, Cardiff, S. Glam.

Welsh Salmon & Trout Association
(previously Welsh Fly Fishing Association)
Swyn Teifi, Pontrhyferdegaid, Ystrad Mewig,
Tregaron, Dyfed.

SPECIMEN GROUPS

National Association of Specialist Anglers
20 Grampian Rd., Stourbridge,
W. Mids. DY8 4UE.

Barbel Catchers Club
26 Chapman Close, Riverview, Kempston, Beds.

Bass Anglers Sportfishing Society
63 Firgrove Rd., Freemantle,
Southampton SO1 3DU.

British Carp Study Group
Heywood House, Pill, Bristol, Avon BS20 0AE.

British Conger Club
5 Hill Crest, Mannamead, Plymouth,
Devon PL3 4RW.

Carp Anglers' Association
Heywood House, Pill, Bristol, Avon BS20 0AE.

Chub Study Group
Fieldings, Manston, nr. Sturminster Newton,
Dorset.

Shark Angling Club of Great Britain
The Quay, East Looe, Cornwall PL13 1DX.

The Tenchfishers
21 Sulgrave Avenue, Poynton, Stockport,
Cheshire.

Inland Waterways Association
114 Regents Park Rd., London NW1 8UQ.